AF837550

I WAS ONCE LOST, BUT I FOUND GOD

My Mental Health Journey Through Pain, Healing & Purpose

Marlon D. Qualls Jr.

Copyright © *Marlon D. Qualls Jr*, 2026
All Rights Reserved

This book is subject to the condition that no part of this book is to be reproduced, transmitted in any form or means; electronic or mechanical, stored in a retrieval system, photocopied, recorded, scanned, or otherwise. Any of these actions require the proper written permission of the author.

Table of Contents

Acknowledgements

I want to thank God for being present in the questions, the silence, and the slow rebuilding. For staying close when faith felt fragile, and for reminding me that grace does not disappear in pain.

Thank you to my family, friends, therapists, and community, those who checked in, prayed, sat beside me, and never made me feel like my pain was too much. Your patience, love, and belief carried me through moments I couldn't carry myself.

And to every person who trusted me with their story along the way: this book carries pieces of your courage, too. May you see yourself in these pages and know that your honesty mattered.

Dedication

This book is for God, who met me in the dark and stayed when I questioned, doubted, and unraveled. For the grace that held me when faith felt fragile, and for the quiet strength that carried me through moments I didn't think I'd survive.

It is also for every version of me, and for you, who chose to stay, to breathe, and to believe that healing was still possible. May these pages be a reminder that surviving was never a failure, and that you were never alone.

To my grandmother and the loved ones who walked before me, this strength is yours too. And to the people who held me up when I couldn't stand on my own.

Trigger Warning

This book discusses mental illness, grief, loss, depression, anxiety, and faith during difficult seasons. It also references suicidal thoughts, attempted suicide and emotional distress. Some passages may be triggering or heavy for certain readers. Please read at your own pace, take breaks when needed, and prioritize your well-being. These topics may be distressing for some readers. Please proceed with care and seek support if needed.

CHAPTER ONE

The Day My Soul Died

Leading to the day my grandma transitioned. The moment grief cracked open my world.

CHAPTER ONE: The Day My Soul Died

Leading to the day my grandma transitioned. The moment grief cracked open my world.

The Hospital

It was October 10, 2016. My grandma got rushed to Methodist South Hospital in Da Haven. She got rushed there because she couldn't breathe. They said she had a mass on her thyroid or something like that, which was making it hard for her to breathe, and she had been hoarse a lot.

Me, really thinking, "Mane, my grandma is strong. She is gone beat whatever it is, like she always does." Every time she went to the hospital, she always came back home, so I had no worries. They transported her from Methodist South on October 11th to Methodist University Hospital, where the specialists she needed were. She was there from October 11th to the 18th. Me again: "Aw yea, my grandma is gonna be good. She's gonna get the help she needs so she can come back home."

Then my grandma got put on life support. Why? I still don't know that reason right til this day. I know she had trouble breathing and was constantly having seizures, so that could've been the reason. In my mind, in my 16-year-old mind, I had sooo much faith in God and believed my grandma was gone come off life support (which she did) and make it home (she didn't).

The Last Day

On October 18th, I stayed out of school to be at the hospital with my grandma. To be exact, Tuesday, October 18, 2016. I was in the room, sitting on the couch, watching my grandma breathe with all the tubes down her throat and nose, something I saw the whole time she was there. I spent my whole fall break beside my grandma… whew, man, I can't get that out of my head.

Her breathing started to get better without the ventilator, so they took the tubes out. My grandma was still asleep, so I ate the food I had brought with me. I'll never forget my mama had cooked pot roast and potatoes. I ate, then took a nap.

I woke up because I heard my grandma trying to get her arms loose. The nurses had strapped them down so she wouldn't pull out the IVs. I went to the bed, and my grandma looked at me and wanted some water, but she couldn't drink or eat anything because her doctor had a test to do on her throat. I said, "Grandma, you can't get none to drink until you take your last test." My grandma started crying. I asked, "Grandma, what's wrong?" She shook her head, saying "nothing."

Man, that broke my heart still breaks my heart every time I think about it because I feel like my grandma wanted to tell me something. I rode that journey out with my grandma, getting out of the hospital. A few hours went by, around 8 or 9 o'clock, they removed my grandma from the ICU floor to a regular floor because she was doing a lot better. I'm talking about up, breathing on her own, talking, knowing how long she'd been in the hospital, and her vitals were all normal.

My sister and I were in the room with my grandma, just talking and happy that grandma was off life support and finna come home. Then my mama and auntie came up, so all of us were just talking and enjoying grandma. My grandma was talking about what she was gone cook when she got home, telling my auntie how she wanted her hair when she got out of the hospital. Man, my grandma was back to her normal self. She said, "I've been in the hospital for 8 days."

The nurse came in and told my mama and auntie that my grandma was doing good, everything looked good, including her vitals, blood pressure, and all. So 10:00 p.m. came, and we were getting ready to leave. My grandma wanted me to spend the night, but I had school since I'd already missed a few days. I swear, that's something I beat myself up about a lot. I wish I would've stayed at the hospital. I honestly feel that she would still be here if I had stayed, or whatever happened that night wouldn't have happened.

As, my mama, sister, and auntie and I got ready to leave, we gave grandma a hug and told her we loved her and we'd see her tomorrow. Oh, rewind when my grandma's husband walked in before we left, my grandma gave a look like she didn't want him there. He hadn't been there all day. Like, what? Now that I'm older, that was a BIG RED FLAG. Only if I had the mindset I have now v.s when I was 16 years old.

The Call

We got home, showered, and got ready for the next day. October 19th was the day my grandma was supposed to take her last test and get discharged. We got home around 11:00 p.m. (October 18th). Around 3 a.m., Wednesday, October 19,

2016, Chocolate (Gloria Taper), who's like a second grandma, has been in the family since before I was even thought of, came in my room screaming, "Jr! Come in here, I think something is wrong with your grandma!" I'm getting up like, "Huh? What?" She said, "Yo mama crying."

So I went to the front where my mama was. My mama was on the couch crying, saying, "They just had to rush mama back to the ICU!" My heart pounded. I asked, "What for?" She didn't know. Then my uncle Wayne called my mama's phone. She handed me the phone because she couldn't talk. I asked him, "What are they saying about Grandma?" He said, "Mama gone, Jr."

I said, "WHAT?!" but then calmed my voice so my mama wouldn't get worked up, 'cause I didn't even tell her that he said she was gone. My heart dropped. I didn't believe it. My mama asked me what Uncle Wayne said, and I told her he said they took Grandma back to the ICU. I didn't know how to tell my mama that, and from the moment he told me, my mind was literally on another planet.

Then my auntie Jennifer pulled up. I walked outside. She was getting out of the car crying. I asked her, "Is Grandma okay?" She didn't say nun. She walked in there with my mama. My mama asked her, "Mama gone?" My auntie shook her head, "Yeah." They just started crying, yelling, and screaming. Man, from that moment, my soul DIED. That 16-year-old me died instantly. I felt my heart and soul leave my body, I swear.

I just felt that same feeling come across me as I write this. I ain't gone lie, that part of me is still dead. No matter what I do or what I accomplish in life, my heart will never be the same. Hell, my life will never be the same. My grandma was my everything.

The Aftermath

Later that morning, October 19, 2016, I woke up from a nap. I went to sleep thinking that when I woke up, it'll all be a dream, but it wasn't. I got on Facebook, and as I scrolled, I saw nothing but posts saying "RIP" to my grandma, with her pictures and long captions. My soul was leaving my body with every post I read, and tears just kept falling.

We ended up going to my grandma's house that morning, and so many family members were there. I'm talking about people who didn't even come to the hospital to visit her. Not even her sisters, and some grandkids, too. It's true, people will drive to you when you are dead, not alive. As I'm walking up the driveway, I'm seeing and picking up on so many spirits and energies. People smiling, laughing… just so much crazy stuff. Man, I'm soulless here. Not saying they are supposed to be crying and sad, but the ones that get me understand what I'm saying. I guess that's our way of coping, huh?

That Saturday, we did a candlelight vigil for my grandma and released balloons. Man, when we released the balloons, and everybody yelled, "RIP Sharon," I couldn't do nothing but cry and say, "My grandma gone." I was soulless, numb, and still couldn't accept it. I still haven't, but I'm healing and getting the understanding.

The Funeral

Leading up to the funeral, I was back at school pushing through, maintaining. Quiet every day, not talking to anybody but my cousins. One day in class, this girl said something about my grandma, and I was finna beat her. All I was hearing was, "Choke her out with both hands around her neck." I'm glad I didn't, because that would've been a charge. That's when I knew I had transformed into a person I didn't know. I just didn't care about life or nothing anymore.

Fast forward to the wake, the viewing of the body. Man, when I walked up to that casket and saw my grandma, I swear I felt my soul and spirit completely walk out of my body. That was the day the reality of not living, just existing, started. I was lost. I wanted to break down and scream, but I couldn't, because of the denial and disbelief. From that day forward, I was completely numb. I died when I saw my grandma lying there. My life had ended. That 16-year-old boy died with her.

The next day, the funeral, I still don't remember much. Everything is still a blur, thank God. All I remember is walking up to the casket with my sister ShanShan. I was numb, no feeling, and she started crying. I told her to "Stop crying," and I felt so bad because she was hurting. She saw Grandma at the hospital the last time I did, but she didn't have a lot of time with her. Her birthday was the last one my grandma celebrated. My baby sister was hurting. I'm sorry, ShanShan, I didn't know how to accept or feel my pain at that moment.

Then, with my brother BellBell being in jail at the time and not being able to make the funeral, that was another hurt. Especially lying to him when he called asking how grandma was doing, I'm telling him she was good when she was dead the whole time. That was a heartache. BellBell, I'm sorry, I just didn't know what to tell you or how to.

After the funeral came the repast, and I was asking everybody, "Why are we doing a repast? What is it to celebrate?" I was just so out of touch with life and reality. I wanted to be with my grandma. It was like people were glad she was gone. There were two different repasts her husband at the time (who I think had something to do with her death) had one at the house with his family, where they took dishes and probably other stuff from my grandma's house. Then our family, the real family, had another repast. Everything was just so off, mane. I can still feel what I was feeling then.

The Darkness

So many days after the funeral, I came home every day after school, just in my room in the dark, with my grandma's pictures all on the wall. I cried daily and didn't talk about anything I was feeling or thinking. My grandma was the first person I lost close to me, and in the Black community, we don't grieve properly or go to therapy. I really didn't have anybody. Nobody was there for me or checked on me but my God, Mama Brenda Savage. I don't know what I would do without her or where I'd be. Lord knows she's one of the reasons that I found God.

My God, Mama worked at my school as a cafeteria manager, so every day after school, I'd go back there with her. We'd pray, and she'd comfort me. Lord, she was and still is my BIGGEST supporter. I love her, and I'm thankful for her.

Fast forward, I started getting suspended and into fights, which wasn't me at all. But that's to say, "Pain turns into anger if the pain isn't dealt with." I hit this boy at one of our basketball games, all because he replied to a comment of mine on Facebook. I just needed to take my anger out on somebody. Hurt people hurt people, even innocent people, to that Boy. I'm sorry, bro. You didn't deserve that. I was full of undealt with grief and was surrounded by people who led me on that night.

The Holidays

Here we are, Thanksgiving, the first Thanksgiving without my grandma. It felt so weird and not normal, because every holiday we were at her house. Being home just wasn't it. Like, is this really my life now? Where is Grandma? The family came over, but my grandma was missing. She would've stopped by for a minute, and we would've gone to her house later, but none of that happened. So I was pretty much to myself, just crying, numb, and stuck.

During Thanksgiving break, it was so painful to be in the house every day and not be at my grandma's. Fast forward to December and Christmas break, the first Christmas without my grandma. Man, it was so hard. I didn't know how I was going to make it through. Life had changed so much that it didn't even feel real or normal. I would've been over to my grandma's house for Christmas break and Christmas Day.

Christmas was her favorite holiday. She used to drink her eggnog, and I used to sneak and drink it too. We used to decorate the house. Mane, just so much was different. Every day I sat around waiting, just knowing my grandma was finna call or walk through the door. And every day that didn't happen, my heart broke even more, but my denial grew stronger.

CHAPTER TWO

Heavy At Sixteen

Living with loss while still trying to grow up.
The silence. The sadness.

CHAPTER TWO: Heavy At Sixteen

Living with loss while still trying to grow up. The silence. The sadness.

When the House Felt Empty

As the holidays went by and it was still Christmas break, some cousins and I decided to go stay at my grandma's house. It was me, three cousins, my grandma's husband at the time, and my uncle twin (Ronald) at the house.

Mane, waking up in that house was different. Waking up and not smelling breakfast, not hearing her voice, her blues playing, or even her waking me up, saying, "Come eat, baby, then go back to sleep." Mane, that was a heartache. But in my head, I'm thinking my grandma was gon' walk through that door at any given moment.

I kept thinking and telling myself my grandma just needed a break from the family, 'cause she was everybody's go-to person. I wouldn't blame her, everybody came to her when they had problems, money issues, food, a place to stay… mane, just a lot. That was too much for one person, especially when nobody checked on her to make sure she was good.

My grandma could be a day out of the hospital, and people would still come to her with their problems. Mane, from morning until the sun went down, I was waiting on my grandma to walk in. When the night came, I'd tell myself, "She'll be home tomorrow." The denial was real, I swear I ain't never been so in denial about nothing.

The Pain That Ain't Make Sense

Another thing that was heavy on me was that we really didn't know what happened to my grandma. She went from doing good, made it off life support, talking, breathing on her own, and was supposed to be released the next day, then all of a sudden she's gone. That just didn't sit right with me, and it still doesn't 'til this day.

I haven't even read my grandma's death certificate, 'cause whatever it says on there I don't think happened. I have been feeling like this since I was sixteen years old. God and I had some ups and downs, and built a strong relationship, but the feeling that my grandma was killed hasn't left my heart. Still, I'm trusting God through it all for peace, understanding, and clarity along the way.

A New Year, No Grandma

January 2017, a new year without my grandma. Life felt so fake, like a dream every day. I'm talking about all my days were blurry, dark, heavy, lonely, and full of pain in my chest.

There were times I wanted to cry but couldn't. Sometimes I'd be lost in a daze, trying to wrap my head around it all. I would call my grandma's phone and get no answer; that broke me all the way down. My grandma always answered my calls. I used to talk to her every day. Even at school, I'd call to ask if she took her medicine.

My life had just changed; I'm talking about a whole 360. I died at sixteen years old mentally… my soul too. My childhood was gone. I had to fight every day just to survive, to live, and to figure out what I was dealing with and what I was feeling.

I was new to death, new to grief, depression, suicidal thoughts mane, and nobody checked in on me. Everybody in my family was smoking and drinking to cope and grieve. I didn't smoke or drink, yet around that time. Some days I'd be in my room lying in the dark, wishing that when I went to sleep I didn't wake up the next morning… just so I could be with my grandma again.

The Birthday I Didn't Want

February came, my birthday month. I had no plans. I didn't want anything, I didn't wanna do anything. I just wanted my grandma. Me being with her in heaven was all I wanted. I put a picture of her and me on my birthday cake.

It felt so different not getting that first phone call of the day, her saying, "Happy birthday, JuneJune." Every year, she was always the first to call me.

Every day was a dark battle. I didn't wanna live at all, man. My life was full of confusion. I was lost and wanted answers to the question: "Why my grandma?"

I was in a place daily, like I was sleepwalking and dreaming through my whole life. My daily routine was school, home and then my room in the dark. I didn't even like to go anywhere 'cause whenever we left home, we always went over to my grandma's house. Leaving the house even started to feel weird.

The Night I Started Questioning Everything

Spring break came, so my cousins and I went back to my grandma's, 'cause that's where all the grandkids were at every school break. Still no show of my grandma, but in my mind, I felt like she was gon' walk through that door… and it never happened.

That's when things had me thinking and questioning my grandma's husband at the time. One night, my cousin and I were in the dining room watching TV when he walked in, and a lady walked through the door behind him. I'm looking like, "Who the hell is this lady?"

Mind you, it's March, five months since my grandma has been gone, and you already moved on this soon? Now I'm wondering, "Did this mane kill my grandma?" My grandma was highly upset at something because dishes would fly off the countertop, and the toilet seat in her room would slam constantly. Aw, she didn't give it a break.

My mama (Shany) and my aunties (Jackie and Jennifer) requested an autopsy when my grandma first transitioned, but her husband canceled it! Like what? You don't wanna know what happened to your wife? That then brought suspicion. That weighed heavy on me.

As the months went by, I still felt the same. Dead, empty, dark. Just going with the flow of my new life, trying to adapt.

The Dream That Felt Too Real

It's now August, my grandma's birthday month. In my head, I'm thinking, "Aw yeah, my grandma finna come home.

She's been gone from her kids and grandkids for almost a year."

Mane, I didn't see my grandma physically, but I saw her in my dream. It felt so real, man. She hugged me, and I told her, "I miss you, Grandma," and she said, "I miss you too." Mane, I woke up crying so hard 'cause I thought my grandma was back. That dream felt so real.

When Reality Hit Me Hard

October 18 came, a day before the one-year anniversary. It really started hitting me that day, 'cause the 18th was the last time I saw my grandma and spent time with her.

In my little denial head, I kept thinking, "Grandma will be back tomorrow when it marks a year. She just needed a break and some time away from this stressful family."

Mane, we did a candlelight vigil at my grandma's house. I went into her room and saw that her clothes had been worn, I kinda tweaked 'cause this mane really had another lady wearing my grandma's clothes.

That candlelight was hard, 'cause that's when it really hit me, my grandma ain't coming back. That's when my grief journey really started.

A whole year later. A whole year of denial. That's when grief, anger, rage, depression, heartbreak, pain, and darkness really took over. I didn't care about anything anymore. I really didn't care to live.

The Same Holidays, Different Pain

Then came the holidays again, Thanksgiving, Christmas. Everything was like a repeat of 2016, but this time I was actually grieving. The denial wasn't the same. I was just learning how to live and keep going with what my life was now.

Thanksgiving came dressed in familiar smells, turkey, greens, dressing and her sweet potato pies in the oven. Christmas followed with lights on the tree and music playing softly in the background.

From the outside, nothing had changed.

But inside, everything had died.

Her chair sat empty, and somehow that empty space was louder than all the laughter in the room. Conversations floated through the house, but they didn't land the same way. The warmth that used to wrap itself around all of us felt thinner, like a blanket that no longer reached our feet.

I didn't just miss my grandma. I missed the feeling she created when we were all together. It's a feeling that I haven't felt since.

She was the glue. The quiet center. The one who made sure everyone showed up, ate well, and felt seen. She remembered the small things, who liked greens the most, who needed to take food home, who was going through something but didn't want to say it out loud. She had a way of moving through the room that made the house feel full, even before everyone arrived.

After she was gone, the gatherings did stop, and they shifted to everybody doing their own gatherings with whom they wanted to gather with.

People came later. Left earlier. Some stopped coming at all. The conversations stayed safe and surface-level. Laughter didn't linger as long. It wasn't that we didn't love each other anymore, well, not quite cause a lot of true colors came out when grandma left, the love and bonds that were once shared WILL NEVER be the same. But it was the person who held us together, who bridged the gaps and softened the edges, who wasn't there to do it.

I used to think families fell apart because of big arguments or dramatic endings.

Sometimes families change simply because the heart of them stops beating.

Grief during the holidays is a quiet kind of heartbreak. The world is celebrating, decorating and posting pictures of perfect tables and smiling faces. And you're standing in the middle of it all, trying to ignore the lump in your throat because someone who should be there isn't.

You laugh at a joke, and then feel guilty because she would have laughed louder. You take a plate of food and remember how hers always tasted better. You look around the room and realize that even though it's full of people, it feels emptier than ever.

There's a special kind of pain in pretending to be okay during a season that tells you to be joyful.

Some moments hit harder than others. Watching someone else stand in the kitchen where she used to be. Hearing a holiday song she loved. Reaching for your phone before remembering there's no one on the other end to call. Grief sneaks up on you in ordinary seconds and turns them heavy.

I prayed differently during those holidays.

Not polished prayers. Not the kind you say out loud at dinner. The kind you whisper in the quiet when your chest feels tight, and the house feels too loud at the same time. I didn't understand why God would take the one person who made our family feel whole. I didn't understand why the holidays had to carry so much ache.

But somewhere in the middle of missing her, I started to notice something.

Love like hers doesn't disappear. It leaves traces.

Maybe that's how God lets love live on. Not by removing the pain, but by planting pieces of the person we lost inside the people who remain.

Still, the truth remains: when my grandma died, something in our family died too. The rhythm changed. The closeness shifted. The holidays became a reminder of both how good it used to be and how deeply we feel her absence now.

The same holidays come every year. The same calendar dates. The same decorations pulled out of storage.

But now they carry different weights.

They carry memories.

They carry longing.

They carry love that has nowhere to land, the way it used to.

And maybe that's what grief really is during the holidays, learning how to hold joy and sorrow in the same hands. Learning how to sit at a table that looks familiar while your heart quietly aches for one more "I love you" from her lips, one more hug at the door, one more "baby" spoken in the way only she could say it.

The holidays will never be the same.

But neither am I.

And every time I showed up, every time I gathered, every time I tried to love my family with even a fraction of the warmth she gave us, I carried her with me.

The pain I never talked about or really dealt with turned into anger. I was getting into fights just to release some kind of pain. After a fight I had at one of the school games, that's when I had my first symptom of Broken Heart Syndrome, and I realized this about three years ago.

Christmas 2017, all I asked God for was to take my life. There were times I'd sleep my whole day away, wishing and hoping I didn't wake up. But I'm still here, so it's definitely a purpose for me to be here, and I'm living that purpose. This book is proof.

To anyone who relates to me or has had any experiences like me in this chapter: keep fighting and don't give up! You made it this far for a reason. You have a reason and a purpose to be here.

This world is a better place with you and me in it.

I Love You,

Marlon Qualls Jr.

CHAPTER THREE

When Grief Got Physical

Broken heart syndrome. The ER. The surgery.
Feeling like my body gave into my emotions.

CHAPTER THREE: When Grief Got Physical

Broken heart syndrome. The ER. The surgery. Feeling like my body gave into my emotions.

Life Got Real

Mane, this is when life got real, and I really had to decide if I really wanted to die or live. I'll say around March 2018 was when I first started to acknowledge the broken heart syndrome symptoms, but I never said anything at all, 'cause I didn't think anything of it myself. It was this one particular day, just a regular day. I came home from school, got in bed watching Empire. I wasn't doing nothing at all, just sitting up in the bed, back against the headboard, watching TV.

My heart started beating so fast for a good 5–10 seconds. I felt a little lightheaded, chest pains, and had a heat flash on my forehead. The heart palpitations stopped, and I felt back normal again. I would get those symptoms a good 3–4 times a day, even at school. The symptoms didn't come back-to-back; they came like every few hours. So I'm having these symptoms every day, but I never said anything, never mentioned it to anyone. Again, I didn't think anything of it at all.

The Scary Day at Votech

I'll never forget the day, it was April 3, 2018. I'm sitting at the table in Votech Culinary Arts Class (I really took that class to eat, by the way). Mane, I'm sitting at the table, and here come these heart palpitations. They started off light, I still didn't say anything. Then all of a sudden, my heart started beating faster than it ever did, I'm talking about 100 mph. My shirt was rising with every heartbeat; the beat was that hard.

I'm having chest pains, and my forehead was dripping sweat like I had ran 5 laps. I turn around and tell the teacher I'm having chest pains. This man looked at my chest and told me, "Aw, bro, you finna die." Don't get me wrong, I was a class clown at Votech, so he probably thought I was playing. I walked out the classroom, went to the office, and told them.

They called the paramedics and my mama. Mane, my mama beat the paramedics there. She's panicking 'cause she sees how my heart is beating and how short of breath I am. I thought I was having a heart attack. My mama ended up seeing the paramedics as we were going down the street, and she stopped them. They got me out of the truck, rushed me on the stretcher, and put me in the back of the ambulance. They checked my blood pressure, put me on a heart monitor and IVs.

My heart rate was 190 bpm. The doctor said if I didn't make it to the hospital in time, my heart could've burst. It was so bad that they set my heart doctor appointment for the very next day. Thanks to my grandma, Brenda Qualls, for advising them to send me to Stern Cardiovascular (Doc McGrew).

Facing Surgery

The next day at the heart doctor, they ran a lot of tests, bloodwork, EKG, heart ultrasound, and asked me how long I have been having the symptoms. I was honest with Doc

McGrew and told him I'd been having them for about a month straight and been grieving heavily over my grandma.

I got all my results back that same day, about an hour or two after the tests. My heart doctor required that I wear a heart monitor to keep track of how my heart performs while at school, sleep, and throughout my day. I'm like, "Okay cool, anything to save my life."

Then I got my results back from the heart ultrasound. There were 2 nerve blockages on my heart that were interrupting blood flow and causing the palpitations. He said, "Mr. Qualls, you have three options: we can put in a stent, a pacemaker, or you can have surgery." To open the blocked arteries and correct the abnormal heart rhythms.

I was nervous, man. I didn't want either of the three. The word *surgery* scares anybody, but I didn't want a stent or pacemaker for the rest of my life. So I told him, "Doc, I'll do the surgery, but I really don't want that either." But I had to do what was best to save the life I thought I didn't wanna live.

Walking with a Heart Monitor

Doc McGrew explained the surgery to me, and it didn't sound too bad. The name of the procedure was "Cardiac Catheterization" surgery. The surgery was scheduled for June 16, 2018. I'm back at school with a heart monitor on, feeling so much less of a person. I'm like, "Ain't nobody else my age going through this, why me?"

Mane, I'm going to school every day with a heart monitor on, and every time I had an irregular heartbeat (also known as an arrhythmia), the heart monitor would beep, and I'd have to step out of the classroom. One of the most embarrassing things ever. I really wanted to just give up, but what kept me going was my mama fighting through it with me. I couldn't give up on my mama when she was with me every step of the way.

I also had others too, my brother, sister, daddy, granddaddy, grandma, Godmama, aunties, and a few others. I had people there by my side, so I couldn't give up on them when they didn't give up on me.

Prom, Loss, and Graduation Pain

It was hard for me to go to prom, graduation practice, and even attending graduation with a heart monitor on. Prom was tough, getting dressed and walking out of the house, not hearing my grandma Sharon's voice. That broke me down. I couldn't even cry or release my emotions how I wanted to, I didn't wanna get myself worked up or put stress on my heart.

Prom night came, I got myself together and took pics with everybody. I went to prom, but honestly, I didn't enjoy it. Oakhaven High Prom 2018 was lame. I hate that we spent that money. Then, in the midst of being on a heart monitor, I lost my favorite auntie, my grandma Sharon's sister, Marylin. That hurt badly; she wasn't gonna be at my graduation.

May came, and graduation was around the corner. Surgery next month (June). I'm nervous about surgery and grieving 'cause my grandma ain't gonna be at graduation, a day we always talked about. May 19th came, graduation day, and not getting a call or even seeing my grandma? That was a broken heart full of pain.

I was on stage, heart pounding, wanting to cry so bad, but holding it together the entire time. Life felt unreal and unfair. I had to do things to keep my mind off my grandma and auntie so I wouldn't add no more stress to my heart.

The Surgery Day

June came fast. I had another heart doctor appointment and finally got off the heart monitor. The doctor gave me all the information for the surgery day. The morning of June 16th, I had to be at the hospital at 5 a.m. Mane, as I'm walking through the hospital, I'm nervous, I'm shaking like crazy. I ain't never been that scared in my life.

My support system was right there by my side. I ain't gonna lie, an old friend I used to call my brother was there every step of the way too, and I still appreciate that. We're sitting in the waiting room, the doctors come to get me to prepare for surgery. My mama and brother look sad, and I'm scared. The surgeons ask if I'm ready. I hit them with the "NOPE." They said, "Well, it's time," laughing.

My family prayed before they took me to surgery. Mane, when they came in that room to get me, I started shaking so bad. I was terrified. I make it to the operating room, all I remember is counting to "3," and nothing else after that.

Learning to Walk Again

When I woke up from surgery, I saw all my folks in the room, even people who weren't there before I went to surgery. The love was real. I was in so much pain. My mama was emotional 'cause the surgery took longer than expected; it was supposed to be 3 hours, but ended up being 5. They found 3 more nerve blockages during surgery, so it was a total of 5.

A few hours later, the doctors requested that I get out of bed and walk around. Mane, I couldn't even stand on my own. That had all of us concerned. The doctors or nurses never told me that I was gonna have to learn how to walk again. I had to get help to shower and move around.

I was down for a couple of months, but during that time, I had a lot to think about, if I really wanted to die or live. I wanted to just lay around, but my grandma Brenda came over to the house and made me get out of that bed and move around and continue to fight. She cooked me a dinner of all my favorite foods and babied me. Going through heart surgery, I didn't wanna die, I was scared to. I did kinda lose myself in the process. I was 18 years old, having heart surgery, when everybody else my age was good and healthy. Now I know my life's calling and purpose are different.

Finding Purpose

Going through heart surgery and having everybody's support was the most love I'd felt since my grandma left. Ashley (Mookie King Freeman) was the first person to visit me at the house; my aunties Jennifer and Jackie showed up. I love them for life. I got a lot of calls and messages too. My auntie DeeDee called my mama almost every hour, "How is nephew doing?" I love her too. My auntie Jackie didn't miss a beat and was one of the first ones to come to the hospital.

My first heart doctor's appointment after surgery was in 2019, they did stress tests, heart ultrasound, EKG, bloodwork, and everything came back good and normal! God is good. I didn't know then, but now I know the purpose! And the purpose that God has for me is different.

My heart doctor told me to watch what I eat. No red meat, beef, or pork, 'cause it increases the risk of heart disease. When he told me that, I stopped eating beef and pork that same day. I still don't eat it til this day, and it's now 2025. My body feels a lot better, no more migraines, and I have more energy.

Still Here for a Reason

After getting my good results, I was ready to chase my dreams. I was ready to get productive and live, man, 'cause I was down for the rest of 2018. Couldn't go to school, work, or anything. Being stuck in the house wasn't it.

Before I could do anything, I had to wait until my next heart doctor appointment to make sure everything was still looking good. After that visit, everything was still normal. My doctor said I could start back doing my everyday activities, but to pace myself and don't lift anything over 10 pounds.

Thank God, all honor and praise to Him, that I had a successful heart surgery. That was proof that I'm here for a reason. Me writing this book, telling my story, is part of that reason.

Broken heart syndrome (Takotsubo Cardiomyopathy) is REAL! The most common cause is extreme physical or emotional stress, like the death of a loved one or a major argument, which causes sudden weakening of the heart muscle. It mimics a heart attack with symptoms like chest pain and shortness of breath.

Please, please, please! If you or a loved one has recently lost someone and you're having these symptoms or grieving hard, go get your heart checked! It's SERIOUS! I didn't say anything at first, and it got worse over time. It could've been too late. So please, take care of your heart. Take it one day at a time. You are loved, and you deserve to be here.

CHAPTER FOUR

Still Holding On

Pain into Purpose. Holding Onto God's Promises.

CHAPTER FOUR: Still Holding On

Pain into Purpose. Holding Onto God's Promises.

Getting Closer to God

My next step was getting closer to God, getting to know Him, His word and the calling and purpose He has on my life. My grandaddy had joined the church "Greater Harvest". My grandaddy then came to us, saying that we needed to join the church. My first visit to the church, I went down to the altar, and this was my first time meeting Pastor Renardo Ward. I remember his exact words: "You're special, there is something special about you, God has an assignment for you to complete, I don't know what it is, but God has a calling on your life". I'll never forget that moment, and this book is proof of that calling. Pastor Ward saw something in me before I even saw it. I joined the Church that same day. I'm still a member, I just need to get more involved.

We ended up moving a street over from my church, and this one particular Tuesday in September 2019, I went for prayer in the prayer room, as I was walking in, everyone was walking out. I asked, "Am I late?" and Sister Bobbie Jefferson replied, "No, you're not, you're actually right on time". Man, that day was a powerful, much-needed day; we prayed about an hour straight. I walked out feeling lighter, anointed and strengthened.

That was the day God had placed Sister Bobbie Jefferson in my life, from the day we met until now, we still text each other Bible scriptures, affirmations, prayers and motivational messages every morning. I love her. God knew exactly what He was doing when He removed people out of my life and added people that's for my journey to keep me close to Him and His word.

Trying to Live Again

So here we are, heart back normal. I'm ready to live my life, ready to just live man. The first thing I do is go job hunting with my brother and sister-in-law (Keanna). We got a job at a warehouse. I hated that job. I just hated to work for somebody, well, it probably wasn't that, it just wasn't my dream or career job. My dream since I was 12 years old was to be an actor. We got off work one day, and I went home looking up casting calls in Memphis, and luckily, they were filming a Christmas movie, "Christmas at Graceland 2."

I signed up, and I got the background role, mane I got on that set, and it felt like I made it. The director loved me. We filmed for like 2 days and wrapped that up, so I was ready for my next gig. So now I have experience in the acting world. I'm looking up casting calls in Memphis. It was this show, "Bluff City Law", set to film in Memphis, but they already had casting calls open. I went ahead and submitted for that show, and I got booked. I got to set and the call time was 5am, and I was the first person there. I was ready for it all. I didn't care about the time. I filmed 2 episodes of that show and got good camera time on the last episode I filmed.

Wanting Empire & God Making a Way

After filming those projects, I'm back at work, which I hated, I'm on lunch break and I get on Instagram and see the

Empire page announce that Season 6 will be the final season. I was so sad, I was like "mane, I'm never going to get a chance to be a part of Empire, I'm never going to meet Taraji P. Henson, Terrence Howard and the rest of the cast." I remember sharing an Empire promo post that Taraji posted. I shared it, saying, "I'll be working with her soon."

Around this time, we had left the job. Now I'm unemployed, I'm sending Instagram DM's to everybody that's affiliated with Empire about being on the show, nobody responded. I found this extras casting guy whose name was Mikey. I'll never forget his name. He changed my life and made my dream come true. I remember him asking me if I was available on a Wednesday. I said "Yes", knowing I'm broke and unemployed. But God, my mama, Pastor Ward and my granddaddy made sure I got there.

My Mama Making the Sacrifice

A MOTHER!! A Mother will risk it all for her children! We were in the middle of getting evicted because my mama was taking the company we were renting from to court. The house we were staying in had flooded, caught fire and molded downstairs in the basement area. They didn't want to fix anything. We were getting sick, so no rent was paid. Long story short, in the middle of going through all of that and trying to find somewhere else to stay, my mama paid the little money she had at the time to make sure I made it to the set of Empire.

When I make it to those places God and I talk about, I owe my mama BIG TIME! I'm connected to people from Empire and get a lot of opportunities because of Empire on my resume. If it wasn't for my mama, granddaddy and Pastor Ward, it wouldn't have been possible. I'm gone, make sure all of them are good!

My First Day on Empire

My grandaddy and I caught the bus to Chicago, where Empire filmed. The call time was like 5pm cause it was a night scene we filmed. Mane, it was so cold, I think it was like 20 degrees, mind you, it's Chicago. So the director put all of us extras in position and gave us the breakdown on how the scene was gonna go. So mane, I'm standing on the sidewalk freezing cold. I saw a black truck pull up, and I started shaking, saying, "omg, this gotta be Taraji." She must've stepped out of that truck, and I said, "OMG! God, I thank you so much, God, you are so real." I was so shocked it felt so unreal that I was there. We wrap that scene up, so we walk back into the hospital we were filming at, and mane, as I'm walking up the stairs, it's THE TARAJI P. HENSON. I got so nervous I whispered, "Hey Taraji", she must've turned around and said, "Hey baby, how are you?" I was DONE! My heart had dropped to my balls, I couldn't believe it.

Getting Booked Again

When I left the set, I went back to the hotel. As soon as I walked in the room, I got an email from Empire asking my availability for another episode. I instantly replied with a quick YES cause hell yea, this, working on Empire is my dream job. I have been wanting to be on Empire since 2015, the second episode, Empire was the reason I went out of town for the first time that I could remember at a big age, Empire was the reason for a lot of my firsts. So I'm back in Chicago by myself this time, I'm walking around exploring downtown, just finally living for a bit after all that life has thrown at me.

Season 6 Episode 10 — The Shot With Taraji

I'm back on the set of Empire. I'll never forget it was Season 6 Episode 10. This episode is so special because I'm in a shot with Taraji, and what's so beautiful and special is that after Taraji and Terrence Howard filmed a scene, Taraji came and stood right next to me. Again, I'm nervous like never before because it still feels so unreal, like I'm really on the set of Empire. I looked at her and said, "Hey Taraji." She said, "Hey baby, how are you? Your hair looks good and healthy." I was saying to myself, God, this can't be real, I'm here. I thank you God for answering my prayers.

They took care of me on set. It was Halloween weekend, and they gave me so much candy, snacks and food. I can go on and on about my Empire journey, but to sum it up, I got booked for several episodes and ended up getting a 3-line speaking role, but COVID came, and production got shut down. Mane, I was so heartbroken.

The Car Wreck

So now I'm back in Memphis from Chicago, because COVID shut down production. My homegirl, Domeneke, was having issues with her mama, so she called me and asked to help her move some of her stuff. I was like, okay cool cause she comes through for me when I need her. We loaded her backseat with all her stuff, me and my lil sister ShanShan was sitting in the front passenger seat. I'm playing gospel music, "You Will Win" by *Jekalyn Carr.* We were riding down the street, and my homegirl must've ran the red light, and the truck hit us from the side, and the car was spinning. We ended up on the opposite side of the road. It happened so fast, all I could do was be my lil sister's shield. I left the wreck with a deep cut on my forehead and had to get 16 stitches. I used to hate the scar, but now I embrace it. It's a survival scar. God was with me cause the enemy was out to get me. I was the only one hurt; my God said not today. I knew then I was under attack and that I was chosen, and ever since then, I have been challenged.

COVID, Grief, and Breaking Down

All of this around COVID, production shutting down for Empire, and the world on lockdown. I had nothing but time to sit with self and mane when I say so much grief, trauma and things that I never talked about had come down on me. It was so much that I had swept under the rug and just worked worked worked and took every gig or opportunity that was presented to me to run from my thoughts, feelings and emotions, really just a lot I didn't wanna feel or deal with. That's why I always say, "If you don't deal with your grief, trauma or whatever it is that you're running from or trying to escape from, it will deal with you."

It's August 8th now, I'll never forget 2020, my grandma Sharon's birthday. We did a lil get together at the park. I ended up getting back cool with a person who back I had 100%. Ion think a person showed up for me how I showed up for them, but that's a story for later in the next chapters. Me, my mama, and auntie Tammy were sitting in the truck talking about the good times with my grandma. I'm feeling weight on my heart because every time my grandma is mentioned, it hits me all over again like mane my grandma is really gone. Later that night, my grandma came to me in my dream. She told me how much she loved me and hugged me, and that shows me that she's still with me.

The Day Auntie Tammy Died

Fast forward to September 30, 2020, a day I'll never forget, mane you just never know when it's the last time. My mama, auntie Tammy, my brother Bellbell and sister Shanshan had just picked me up from work. We were sitting on the hotel lot where my auntie Tammy was staying. Mane, we were out playing, kicking it and planning my mama's birthday on how we're going to surprise her. As we were getting ready to leave, my mama truck wouldn't crank up. We were sitting out there for about 3 hours, I guess that was to spend more time with her.

We finally left. I went home and left to spend a night over a friend's house. I went to work the next morning on October 1st at 6am. Mane, when I say I was feeling so weird, I'm at work running off back and forth to the restroom, I had the nervous feeling that something was off. I went to the restroom cause I had received a text from my cousin asking if I had talked to my mama. I replied, "yea", she asked me, "she told you about Tammy?" My heart dropped because "huh?" I called my mama and she answered the phone crying, telling me what happened and that they were on the scene. I leave work and get to the scene and man, that broke my heart to see my auntie laying on that ground like that, bloody. My auntie was shot in the neck, that crushed me, and sometimes I still don't believe she's gone cause we saw her almost every day.

My Anxiety Attack at the Wake

Seeing my mama hurt and broken, that's something that gets to me right to this day cause my mama is still torn up about that, her and my auntie did everything together. When my mama's car was down, they were walking together. Auntie Tammy wasn't my mama's blood sister, but they were closer than most; you couldn't tell them they weren't blood sisters, blood couldn't make them closer. I still see the pain in my mama's face about her, nobody coming as REAL as Auntie Tammy, they were ride or die. Here we are at the wake.

When I walked up to that casket and saw my auntie, that crushed my heart. My body went numb! She did not look like herself! As I was walking out, my legs started tingling. I didn't say anything cause I didn't think anything of it, but my heart was heavy. When we stepped outside, numbness shot up from my legs up to my upper body. I told the person I was standing next to that I couldn't move. My body started to tighten up, and I started to get shortness of breath. My face started tightening up, and my hands were locked. I thought I was having a stroke. My auntie Jackie was yelling, "he's having an anxiety attack, y'all" My auntie was telling me to breathe slow and to stay calm because I was scared because I thought I was dying. They rushed me to the hospital, and they couldn't even find the reason or couldn't even tell me what it was.

Pills, Panic, and Edibles

The doctor gave me some Xanax for anxiety and to sleep. Those pills had me dreaming about my auntie Tammy and a lot of other things. I woke up out of my sleep cause I started having another anxiety attack in my sleep. I got rushed to the hospital again. This time I thought it was the end for me. All I kept saying on the way there was "I don't wanna die". It felt like my chest was caving in. When I got to the hospital, they still couldn't find what was going on. I just had to deal with grief, man. That's when I started eating edibles. Mind you, I didn't smoke at all, I didn't use any kind of drugs/THC, I was just a drinker and not a heavy one. I started the edibles and loved the feeling it gave me, the escape from the world, the numbness to certain thoughts and feelings, literally on another planet. The grief and state of mind I was in at the time, I just wanted peace, mane, and nobody really understood me. It got to the point I just had to find a way to try not to even think about it.

My Mama's Birthday After the Loss

It's November 1, 2020, my mama's birthday and 1 month since the death of Auntie Tammy. Her and my mama had plans, but God had other plans. I just had to do something special for my mama. My auntie Caprice helped me in the process with the party. I told her what I wanted to do, and we made it happen. I wouldn't have made it happen without her. I love her. I decorated the building and had my grandma Sharon and Auntie Tammy's pictures there. My mama was full of pain and hurt, that was a tough one losing her ride or die and before her birthday at that.

Pulling Away & My Pastor Pushing Therapy

After all of that, I kinda felt myself slowly departing from myself, then I had a talk with my Pastor (Renardo Ward). I told him some of the things I was dealing with mentally, and he suggested that I give grief counseling a try and he thought that would help me, and how good of a grief counselor Dr. Sarita was. I've gone to therapy as a child, but I never talked to a therapist or counselor about grief or death, even when I lost my grandma, Sharon. I was like, "Ok, pastor, thank you, I'm gonna reach out to her." Knowing I wasn't going to reach out to the grief counselor, at the time, I felt that talking to somebody about my problems and what I was going through, nobody was going to understand me, nor even care. I felt there was nothing or nobody that could help me. I was using edibles and drinking liquor as my coping methods. That was the only thing helping me feel good, no thoughts nor pain.

Acting Again & Losing My Great Grandma Emma

Fast forward to 2021, I was feeling myself slowly fleeing away from acting, the last project I was working on was Empire, and COVID was still around in 2021. The entertainment industry was still kinda shut down. I started looking up casting calls, doing virtual game show contests, just a lot of things to keep my Empire momentum going. I made an Actors Access account, and they had so many casting calls on there from Tyler Perry projects, really everything. I saw a casting call for this local project, "The Bodyguard" by LaQuita Langhorn. I submitted, got an audition date, nailed the audition and got the role. I'm forever thankful for LaQuita. She gave me my first projects on Tubi, Peacock, Amazon

Prime and other platforms. But we filmed The Bodyguard the summer of 2021, and it was a good experience filming a feature film, which prepared me. Then I lost my great grandma Emma Thompson, and that was something that bothered me, going to a nursing home, having to visit my grandma through a window, and her not really remembering none of us was heartbreaking. When she passed, I couldn't even cry. I still haven't cried. I've lost so many people, I'm numb. So, I eventually started smoking.

Avoiding Family & The Solo Chicago Trip

As it got closer to October 19, my grandma Sharon's death anniversary, I felt myself feeling those feelings from October 2016. I didn't want to be a part of the family gatherings at the cemetery or a candlelight. I knew our family had died when my grandma left is when we did a candlelight the year before, and I had Pastor Ward come out and pray. Pastor Ward had told all of us to hold hands, and mane, it was so many gaps in between people. NOBODY wanted to hold hands, I was like, yeah, this family dead and won't be coming back together. So I did a thing, I booked myself a solo trip to Chicago for the weekend of October 19, 2021. I couldn't be around the fake and hate.

My First Real Therapy Session

I had reached out to Dr. Sarita Wilson and set up a grief counseling session. I was a little nervous and really didn't know what to say. She asked me, "What's been going on?" I replied, "I lost my grandma". Man, I just started crying. I had a good cry that day. I haven't cried like that since it had been a year since my grandma had been gone, and I realized that she wasn't coming back.

I had finally felt that someone understood me, heard me and felt me. Dr. Sarita was so patient with me as I cried and got my emotions out. I first started the session lying to her and having a wall up, but I eventually got honest with her if I wanted therapy to work and if I wanted healing. Every time I didn't tell her how I was really feeling or what I was going through, the weight got heavier and heavier on my heart.

That first session was a good one and helped me a lot. One of the most important things I've learned in therapy is: "In order for therapy to work, you have to be honest with your therapist/counselor."

A Moment of Peace in Chicago

After that session, I left the hotel, went shopping, got me a facial, got my eyebrows waxed and took myself out to dinner. My mental was like 80% cause all I really needed was to talk to somebody who didn't know me, who couldn't judge me or tell me "let's drink or let's smoke" instead of actually talking about what's going on. After I left from eating. I went downtown Chicago and took a walk on the river. My trip came to an end, and as I'm heading back to Memphis, I felt the darkness before I even arrived.

Losing Grandma Betty

When I got back to Memphis, I was really on chill mode and wasn't going anywhere besides hanging with a group of people at the house who weren't good for me. November 18, 2020, I'll never forget. I'm in my room sitting on the couch scrolling Facebook. I saw my cousins changing their profile pics to my grandma Betty Parham. I reached out to see what was going on, and my cousin Tiffany said, "Grandma is on hospice and she has 72 hours to live." Again, I'm numb. I don't know how to feel. I didn't want to see her on hospice on top of losing my grandma Emma a couple months back. I didn't go see her, but I really wouldn't have had a chance cause she died that same night, like an hour after I got the news. All I did was roll up and start smoking. I didn't even wanna think about it. I wish I had more time with her and built a closer bond and relationship, but whenever I went to visit her, she showed me nothing but love. I knew she loved me, and she knew I loved her. She would keep telling me over and over, "Boy, you look just like Michael and your daddy." I miss her a lot.

Losing Jayson, The One That Broke Me the Most

I didn't leave the house after the news of Grandma Betty, besides going to her candlelight. I didn't want to be bothered with nobody at all. November 20, 2020, WHEW BOY MANE! I'll never forget this day. I'm in my room in the bed watching TV, my brother calls my mama, and she puts the phone on speaker. I hear him ask her, "Ma, you heard what just happened to Jay?" I instantly raised up. She said, "Jay who? Wayne's nephew Jay?" My brother said, "yea, it's on Facebook that he just got shot at the mall."

I must've got on Facebook, and as soon as I opened the app, that was the first thing I saw. When I say my heart didn't even feel like it was in my chest, seeing that article that he died didn't even look real. That whole night was like I was alive daydreaming, that's something I didn't feel numb to, I felt every pain it was.

Me and Jay go wayyy back, back to 2007 when my mama and his uncle were dating. You couldn't tell us we weren't brothers/cousins, we went to school together at Evans, celebrated our birthdays together, his birthday February 15 and mine February 16. We have so many memories, mane. We used to stay fighting. I remember when his mama, Chrissy, whooped us for fighting and made us hug for hours, her and my mama then left, and she said: "When we come back y'all still better be hugging". As soon as they left, we stopped hugging. We heard them pulling back up and started back. My mama, Chrissy, Wayne and Arthur walked in saying, "We know y'all ain't been hugging all this time, y'all can tell that to somebody else." They already knew what was up.

So many memories, mane, and what broke me the most was I had just seen him at the store by his house in October before I went to Chicago, I told him I was gonna hit him up when I got back. So imagine that pain my grandma then Jay 2 days apart, losing Jay hit me the hardest. I'm not gone lie that ripped a part of my heart.

December The Hardest Month

November and December were two hard months for me; my grandma's funeral was first in November, then Jay's funeral was last in December. Seeing Jay in that casket BROKE ME. All I could do was cry, all I kept saying to myself, this can't be the Jay I grew up with. This can't be him, no way. That was the most I've cried in a minute, randomly throughout the day and crying myself to sleep; that pain felt like the pain when I lost my grandma Sharon.

But the beautiful part is that his Baby Boy Jaylen (who got shot with him at the mall that was 9 months old at the time) survived and was recovering. I started smoking and drinking heavily, but in December I was smoking almost every hour cause smoking put me in a different world, but no matter how high I got, all I saw was Jay's face and I was still in disbelief.

Trying to Hold Onto God's Promises

In the process, I'm still trying to hold onto God's promises cause my life was just getting back on track, my mental health was getting good, I started grief counseling, and then this happened. I was like "God, this can't be life, I know you ain't doing me like this".

As Christmas approaches, I'm dealing with these new deaths and still grieving and missing my grandma Sharon. I needed her badly cause she would've been the only one to understand me. But losing Jay, my mama, brother, Alex and my God mama was there for me. My mama and brother would get me out of the house, and my God mama would get me out of the house too and was there when I needed to talk and just express how I was feeling. They held me down that November and December. New Year's Eve came, and I got so drunk and high cause everyday, all day, I was hurt and numb but still felt the pain.

Gone on over to chapter 5… This Journey Gets Real!

CHAPTER FIVE

God, Are You Still There?

Wrestling with faith in the dark, Questioning, Doubting, then slowly finding my way back.

CHAPTER FIVE: God, Are You Still There?

Wrestling with faith in the dark, Questioning, Doubting, then slowly finding my way back.

Waking Up in the Dark

It's now January 2022. Here I am waking up every day suffering in silence, smoking my life away. It wasn't a day nor hour I wasn't smoking. I'm up almost every morning at 5 a.m., smoking and listening to Rod Wave. That mane music spoke to my soul, exactly what I was feeling.

I'll never forget this day, January 17, 2022. I'm sick as ever. My mama and I had caught COVID. Imagine grieving and having COVID. That was a tough one. I couldn't breathe out my nose, I'm stuffy, and still trying to smoke to escape grief and thoughts. That same day, Channel 3 News had released Jay mama (Chrissy) interview. She had just broken her silence. Mane, to see "Who Killed Jayson Hill?" on that screen just didn't feel real. Then to see Chrissy on the news crying broke me. It all felt like a dream. No matter how sick I was, I smoked through it all. I just didn't want to feel anything at all.

Once I recovered and got better, I tried to help myself out a little. I applied for a job at FedEx to get myself out of the house so I wouldn't be in my head so much. I got the job and started working that Monday. I had to smoke before work so I could have a peaceful day. When I got to work, I met the supervisor I would be working with. Mane, she came in loud like it's not 8 in the morning, Jenifer Lewis loud. I'm saying to myself, "I got this job for peace of mind, and this is what I signed up for?" I held on to the job for four days. The work was easy; it just wasn't helping me mentally because I was still in my head, still thinking about everything I didn't want to think about.

While I'm working, I'm watching the clock every second, ready to get off to smoke. Some days I would get up for work, pull up to work, get out the car, and before I get to the door, I turn around saying, "I can't do this today. I need my bed and a blunt." There were times I would leave work, go get me a margarita, and go straight to the cemetery to Jay's grave. I would sit at his grave, smoke and drink, then go to my grandma Sharon's grave after because they're buried across from each other. When I leave the graves, I would go home and repeat, smoke, drink, and listen to music all day.

The first six months of 2022 were my darkest ones. I've never been that dark ever in my life. I was so dark, I swear my vision was black and white. I'm still trying to hold on to faith in God until it broke. It felt like God wasn't hearing my prayers or my cries and didn't care what I was dealing with. All I'm asking is, "Why me, God? Why Jay? Why my grandma? What did I do wrong?" I didn't get an answer.

I was just so lost on how, when I started to finally talk to a grief counselor and get my mental health on track in October 2021, then BOOM, I'm hit with all of this at once in November 2021. I doubted that I would ever be okay again. I just knew it was the end for me. What I was feeling and going through, I had never felt like that. I was so dark I couldn't see. I was kinda scared of myself.

Reaching for Help While Losing Hope

This random day, I decided to reach out to my grief counselor, Dr. Sarita, to set up a session. She had availability the next day. We got on Zoom, and she asked me, "How are you doing? I haven't heard from you in a minute." I told her I recently lost my grandma on November 18th, then my cousin Jayson on November 20th, while still grieving my grandma Sharon. She asked me, "How are you feeling?" I told her, "I don't know. I can't even explain it. I wake up every day with no feeling. It's like I'm just existing. I see black and white. I don't see color anymore. It feels like I've escaped from my body."

She told me, "You're numb. You've had so much death back-to-back in such close range, and you haven't had time to deal with them or grieve. You're numb to the pain." I just broke down crying. I was crying a good lil minute because I didn't know who I was anymore, and being numb explained it all. She gave me healthy coping mechanisms to try, and journaling was one of them. I'm gonna be honest, I didn't start journaling right then. I felt smoking and drinking was the only thing best at the time.

February has come, my birthday month, and everybody is asking me what I'm doing for my birthday. My response was nothing at all. In reality, I wanted to be dead, literally, because the place I was in life mentally was hard. My mama said I needed to do something. I kept telling her I was good and didn't want to celebrate, but to make her feel better, I told her we could have a party. She instantly started buying everything for the party, and to be honest, I really didn't want to do the party. So I planned that it would be my *going-away party*. I'm sure y'all know what that means.

It snowed during my birthday week, so I pushed the party to the following weekend. The night of the party, everybody was already there before me, and I'm at home putting my clothes on and writing suicide notes at the same time because I was planning to commit suicide. I figured that would be the best timing, while everybody was gone, just me at home. Then I had to think about my mama, brother, sister, or cousin coming home and finding me like that. So I smoked and cried before they came and picked me up because I really wanted out of life.

I got to the party 2 hours later, and mane, I had a time. I enjoyed myself, and I don't remember the last time I felt that good. Being surrounded by all that love was something I needed. What made the night even better was when Chrissy came. Seeing her was like seeing Jay, him and his mama twins. I felt Jay, my grandma Sharon, and Auntie Tammy there in the spirit. I had all their pictures there side by side.

Later that night, before the party was over, I took pictures with everybody because I was still contemplating committing suicide. When I got home, I sat on the couch in my room and cried as I looked through all the pictures, seeing how many people I would have hurt if I ended my life, especially my mama. Mane, I just couldn't do it, and I didn't want a painful death.

Another Loss I Wasn't Ready For

March 2022, my great grandma Berdie Mae Saulsberry, my mama's dad's (Andrew Saulsberry "Mac Tall") mama. My grandma had dementia, and it had gotten bad. Me and my mama were going over there late at night with her while her caregiver was there as well. About a week later, my grandma ended up going to the hospital. My nerves were so bad because I have PTSD from my loved ones going to the hospital and not making it out. I didn't go visit my grandma at all while she was there. I know that would've taken a deep toll on me mentally.

The family all went to the hospital on March 19 because I think my grandma was transitioning. I went to the hospital, but I sat in the car the entire time. I couldn't see my grandma like that. I knew I couldn't handle that on top of what I was already feeling and going through. What hurt me the most was that I couldn't be there for my mama how I wanted to. People kept coming to me saying, "Yo mama needs you, you gotta be there for her." I'm telling them, "I know, I know, but I can't. What I'm going through and feeling right now, I can't even put my pain to the side and fake it." I needed somebody to be there for me.

I couldn't even be there for myself. The weed was my only go-to. My grandma passed the same night, March 19. When I got the call, I had pulled off the parking lot. I didn't want to see my mama like that. My grandma Berdie Mae was the only mother figure my mama had since my grandma Sharon left. When I got home, I was rolling up in disbelief like, "Lord, not again." I didn't cry. I couldn't cry. I was so numb, but my heart was full of pain.

After my grandma's funeral, I slipped deeper into grief and depression on top of what I was already dealing with. I'm smoking and drinking heavily. I felt so alone, mane. It was people who came to chill with me, but whenever they came, we were smoking and drinking. I started to question, "Are these people even good for me?" I tried to talk to some people about what I was going through, but they started telling me, "Here you go with this depressed stuff." It's like whenever it comes to me grieving, feeling, or even expressing how I felt, I'm not supposed to feel nor grieve. But whenever these same people started to grieve their daddy and grandaddy or whoever, they wanted everybody to feel their pain, hear them, and be there for them. I did all of that and never told them how they should feel.

Then one day, this dude I used to call my brother told me, "I feel like you ain't trying to get over your grandma's death." Like, what? Me going through everything I was going through, I started questioning everybody in my circle. I realized that I was going through my storm alone and went through everybody else's storm with them. What was kind of confusing to me was that I was surrounded by so many people and still felt alone. And that's one of the most difficult, confusing feelings ever, because why are y'all here? Why am I even here? Everybody had to go!

Living on the Edge

Every day was a battle, from January to June, not knowing which day I was gone end my life. It was this one particular day, it was like 9 p.m., I went to the emergency room because I was having chest pains the entire day, and the chest pains didn't stop. The doctor didn't know what was the cause, so I had to set up an appointment with my heart doctor. When I went to the heart doctor, they did a heart ultrasound and an EKG. My results came back normal, but my heart doctor suggested that I wear a heart monitor again to see how my heart performs throughout my day and in my sleep.

I had to stop smoking for that time period while being on the heart monitor, and mane, I was so desperate without smoking because I had to sit and deal with all my thoughts. My heart doctor called on a Friday and said, "Mr. Qualls, everything is looking good. You can now remove the heart monitor." After that call, the first thing I did was thank God and start smoking.

I had told my mama about my heart situation, and she told me, "You need to find yourself." Mane, the anger and rage I felt on the inside. One, because it was true. Two, I didn't know how to because I was never taught how to deal with or take care of my mental health. Us as Black people don't deal with our mental health. I was doing what I saw my family do when they deal with things, and that's smoking and drinking. So what am I supposed to do? Nobody understood me or heard me.

Every day I woke up, my heart was heavy and aching. I was so dark, I saw no way out of that darkness. I was still going to church, trying to give God a try after try, but after one Sunday, I stopped going. I stayed home daily and went to the cemetery about three times a day. There were days when I couldn't sleep at all. I was up one whole week straight, no sleep, just me, weed, and liquor. I didn't know who I was anymore.

When the Voices Got Loud

I'll never forget this one Friday night in May, the suicidal thoughts got loud, and the voices in my head had got LOUDER. It was about 9 p.m. I'm at the house smoking, having a moment, so I decided to go to the cemetery. That's the only time when I felt closer to my grandma and Jay. I'm sitting at Jay's grave, smoking and talking to him, and as I was leaving, mane, I was just rushed with different feelings and emotions. I'm crying, listening to music, and my head is full of voices.

As I'm driving, I'm hearing voices telling me to run off the bridge, run into the back of a 18-wheeler, and to stop the car in the middle of the expressway. I mean, at that time, I wanted to die, but I didn't want a painful death. When I got home, I started smoking. I also started typing my own obituary because this was my last straw. I couldn't take it anymore. I knew it was going to be hard on my mama losing me, so I didn't want to put more on her by preparing an obituary. I'm crying while typing it, then I stopped. Mind you, I'm overwhelmed with all these different feels, emotions, and voices in my head. I'm in a place where I've never been.

I then started hearing different voices telling me to "take the pills, don't take the pills," over and over again. I'm crying so bad because I'm so confused about what to do. I swear I wanted to die, but I didn't want to take myself out. I went in my closet and got a bottle of Benadryl. I poured a handful and threw them in my mouth. I tried to swallow, but I couldn't. I spit the pills out and just started crying. I was like, "God, what do you want from me? If this is what life is going to be about, I want out."

I then fell asleep on the couch in my room, and I felt a movement next to me, like someone had sat down. I didn't wake up just then because the door was locked. Who could be in here? I felt the movement again, and I opened my eyes, and Jay was sitting right next to me. I swear I wasn't dreaming, I was wide awake. I'm looking like, "What are you doing here?" I started crying. He wiped my tears, telling me, "You bsn, bruh. You got things to do. I got you."

Then my grandma walked through my door, and the door was still closed. She said, "Stop crying, JuneJune. Grandma here, I got you." Mane, after that, I cried so hard because they really came to see me. Their skin was so beautiful. They had on all white. I knew I was on the verge. God knew sending them would save me; that's why He sent them.

Finding My Way Back and Seeking Help

From that day forward, I had to get myself together. God knew exactly what I needed. The day after, I took a break from smoking and drinking, and I started back praying and gave God another try. It still felt like God wasn't hearing me, and I even started meditating. I tried so much to change the state of mind I was in, and none of that helped, so I started back drinking and smoking. I felt my best when I was drunk or high. I was so upset with God, he was every name in the book, cause God, where are you? I reached out to my grief counselor to set up a session because I really wanted to put in the work to change my situation. I didn't wanna keep living like that. We did a session on a Thursday, and I asked her if I was bipolar because my mood swings were all over the place. One minute I'm perfectly fine, and the next minute I'm angry and irritated. It really hurt my heart that I went off yelling at my sister when she was only checking on me. She came into my room and asked, "Are you okay?" and I told her, "Leave me the F*** alone and get out of my room" The look on her face crushed me cause all she was doing was checking on her big brother. I went into her room and told her I was sorry, I was just in a bad mood.

When Anxiety Hit

Then, while on this journey of grief and depression, my anxiety started to affect me to the point where I was passing out. I had just come home from the cemetery, my mama and brother sitting at the table talking, and all of a sudden, my head started to tighten up, and my vision was starting to go dim. I told my brother to pass me a water out of the fridge, he asked if I was good cause I only drink one brand of water, and I didn't drink the water I was asking for. I was like, yeah, but my vision getting darker and my head feeling tight, my mama told my brother to help me to the car that she's about to rush me to the fire station. Mane all I remember doing is walking to the kitchen, and the moment I got in front of the stove, everything had just went dark. I don't remember anything after that. I remember waking up in the truck. They had to pour water on me to get me up. When everything went dark, my body felt so cold, and I was in a peaceful state at that moment, but it was so scary.

The Wake-Up Call

That was another sign that I needed to get myself together cause everything that I wasn't really dealing with started to deal with me physically, had my mama scared to sleep at night worrying about me. I was even scared to sleep, not knowing if I was gone wake back up. After that scare, I eventually put the weed and liquor down and rebuilt my relationship with God cause my situation had got worse when I stopped praying. I ended up getting another job because my money was getting low and I had to continue to help my mama on the bills, mane I had lasted at this job a month because this Mexican supervisor thought she was about to talk to me any kind of way. I was still a lil mentally unstable, and once she started picking at me, it was easy for me to blank out. I called her a 304, I said, "y'all better get this 304" because nobody said anything to her when she came in picking at me. Mane, it was voices in my head telling me to put both of my hands around her neck and choke her out, don't stop until she's not breathing anymore. I thank God that I didn't listen to that voice cause that would've been a serious charge.

Back to Old Habits

So when I got fired from that job, I was just sitting at home bored with nothing to do. I started back smoking, but not as crazy as I was earlier in the year. I was hard on myself. I got on Instagram, and I saw Taraji interview on the Breakfast Club talking about Mental Health. When I say I was and still am into every interview of Taraji's because everything that she talks about mental health, I was going through and can relate to. When Taraji broke her silence publicly about mental health, she inspired me to do the same and made me feel lighter knowing that there are more people out in the world fighting the same battles. I no longer felt alone.

Learning Vulnerability

Taraji is the reason I'm so transparent and vulnerable when telling my story publicly or in front of crowds. I am proud to say that my vulnerability came from a woman (Taraji P. Henson) and not a man. Growing up, men used to always say, "Boys don't cry." That's a BIG LIE, not crying, holding all those feels, pain and emotions in, hurts worse than not crying and not releasing. Big thanks to Taraji P. Henson; she helped me when I couldn't help myself, and she will FOREVER have a place in my heart. After watching all of her interviews advocating for mental health and telling her story gave me so much hope, and she is the one who motivated me to tell my story. She always says, "If you have a story to tell, tell it; you never know whose life your story could save." After all of that I went through mentally, I said to myself "Yeah, I gotta tell my story cause I know I'm not the only one going through this." That's when I created my podcast (Express Yourself with Marlon) in my living room. I brought people on the show with similar stories, but the goal was to show that NONE of us are ALONE!

Finding My Way Back

To be honest, when I stepped into the podcast world, for some reason, I smoked before every episode. I still don't know why, but what I can say is that I got it done. When I started Express Yourself with Marlon, I was in the process of finding my way back to me, my relationship with God had gotten better, my heart got lighter, and that darkness was slowly leaving. I went on a press run to promote my podcast's first season, and I did my first TV interview with Gina Neely on her talk show (Bluff City Life with Gina Neely). My life was slowly changing. When my relationship with God got stronger, my mental health started to get better. What I had to learn was that in order for me to get better mentally and physically, I had to do my part and meet God halfway, I had to break my bad habits, I had to be honest with myself grief counselor in order to get the proper help, tools and coping mechanisms that I needed. I am forever thankful for Dr. Sarita. Man, she was so patient with me when I wasn't patient with myself, even when there were times I just cried during a session. She gave me so many tools and helped me understand grief and even myself. It all started with me because God was there and He was hearing me, I just wasn't hearing Him because I was always high and drunk with a cloudy mind.

CHAPTER SIX

Where Was Everyone?

Helping others while feeling alone and isolated.

CHAPTER SIX: Where Was Everyone?

Helping others while feeling alone and isolated.

Whew! Mane, where was everyone? Where was everybody who so-called loved me? Where were those so-called brothers? Where were those so-called friends? Mane, where was everybody I had shown up for?

Showing Up Alone

I supported so many people when they lost loved ones, and all of that love and support I gave out, I didn't receive a bit of it. I barely saw some of them, and I didn't see most of them at all. What kind of hurt me the most was that the people I was there for, listening to them vent, being that shoulder for them to lean on, were the same people telling me they didn't want to hear that depressed stuff, or they felt like I wasn't trying to get over my grandma's death. It seemed like the only time people cared about what I was going through or were willing to hear me vent was when they needed to borrow some money. I'm talking about I'm showing up, supporting people, when I need somebody to show up for me and be in my corner. I literally saw a lot of faces when it was beneficial for them. I went through 85% of my storm alone, suffering with thoughts and voices. I saw so-called brothers and homeboys when it was time to smoke, drink them dealing with money problems or vent about a relationship. When I got rushed to the ER due to a bad anxiety attack, I really had a person who came to the hospital pretended like they were there for me. The whole time, they came up there to ask me for some money to get something to eat. Mane, it's like when I look back, people that were around me and showing up for me were taking advantage of me during my times of grieving. When I didn't use to show up for people at times because of what I was going through, they really used to get mad at me, but everybody else who didn't show up got a pass. It was like what I was going through didn't matter. Mane, it was people out of state who I never met, and some I had met and became close with through social media, who would listen to me vent, cry, listen, or even just check on me. It was a lil hurtful that all of the people I showed up for weren't there for me like I was for them. All I wanted in return was the same love and support I gave out when I needed it most.

When God Was All I Had

But what I can say is that I learned that God will take you through something so dark and painful to show you who is really there for you. He will show you who your people are in times of need, grief, and loneliness. When everybody left me, my God never did. You find out who your people are when you're quiet.

Letting Everybody Go

It came to a point where I just had to let everybody go. One day, my homeboys and I were chilling and smoking. Mane, when they left, I sat back and thought to myself, "This is the only time I see these people, but where are they when I'm up all night with deep, scary thoughts, tears, and can't sleep?" At that moment, I started deleting contacts. I had let everybody go at the same time. I was over it all, and in order for me to heal and grow, I had to let everything and everybody go who wasn't adding to my healing and my growth. In order for me to grow, I had to let go, even when it was hard to.

Expired Seasons

About two days later, the majority of them were calling and texting, worried, asking if I was good, wanting to offer support, but I was ignoring everybody. Everybody's season had expired with me. There were times they'd pop up to my house, and I would watch them on the camera just standing at the door. Cutting all of that dead weight out of my life was one of the best things I've ever done. The moment I did that, my life got better and lighter.

Pouring From an Empty Cup

Something I recognized was that on my healing journey, I was carrying everybody else's problems, filling and pouring into everybody else's cup, while carrying my own problems, and nobody was pouring back into me. I was sharpening everybody until I went dull, and nobody thought to sharpen me.

Isolation, Healing, and God

After I cut all of those people out of my life, I went into isolation, took a social media break, and built a stronger relationship with God. I got back into church, started praying daily, meditating, and just taking care of me, being there for me and giving myself all the love and care I was giving everybody else. While on my journey, I stopped overextending myself. I only showed up when I could or when I felt the need to, especially for the ones who showed up for me. I was still smoking, I'm not gonna lie, but not as heavy as the beginning, and I had let the liquor go. My mental health didn't get back on track fast because I was still being challenged on my healing journey. That was God building character and preparing me for the journey that He had written.

God Mama Brenda Savage

My God, mama, Brenda Savage, was there for me every step of the way, never let me go, and she's still here with me. We'll be on the phone for 5+ hours, she's listening to me, praying for me, and praying with me. I don't know where I would've been without her. God placed her in my life for a reason and a purpose at 12 years old.

My Reason to Stay Alive

My mama Shany, daddy Marlon Sr., Brother BellBell, Sister ShanShan, Grandaddy Andrew Saulsberry, God mama Brenda Savage and my nieces and nephew Kaci, MJ, Maddie and Mackenzie were my reasons for staying alive. I had a vision of my funeral, and I saw all of those faces I would've hurt if I threw in the towel. It was so heavy and dark on my journey. Before I attempted suicide, I had written letters to all of my close loved ones, mane. But I couldn't do anything but think about my nieces and nephew, because they love their Uncle Jr. One day, I was suicidal and was making a video, my niece Kaci walked in with her doll loving on me, which changed my mood. She saved my life that night; who knows what I would have done if she hadn't walked in. I couldn't give up; if I would've given up, I would've let my grandma Sharon down, because she never gave up. On my healing journey, I had to think about all the people that did love me.

Family That Shows Up

One thing about my cousins and my twin, Tiara and Tamara, and Domeneke, they show up for me whenever I call or whenever I have something going on. They know the love I have for them is unmatched. My uncle Herb, too, he gone check in, call, and speak life into his nephew. Unc know I love him. My cousin TRE, one thing about her, she pulled up whenever, no matter the time. We smoked, she let me vent, but told me what needed to be done. I love her for life! I have a lot of cousins named Toya, but this one knows who she is. My fav always came through for me on one call, that's all, I love her. My friend/brother Rodrice gone call or text if he hadn't heard from me in a minute. When I cleared my circle of people, God started sending people I needed, and they came into my life with genuine love, support, and no hidden agendas.

Alex

Alex, I can't leave her out. She was there for me, too, on my journey. There were times we'd sit in the parking lot eating food, just talking. There were times she'd ride out to the cemetery with me late at night. Mane, she rode my journey out with me. She never rushed me off the phone when I was venting for hours. She knows my love for her is forever, and she'll always have a place in my heart.

Jay Gholston (Mad Rich Apparel)

My boy Jay Gholston, he would call, text, and check in on me to make sure I'm straight, and I do the same for him. He just doesn't know how much his strength gives me strength and encourages me, no lie, because he doesn't have to do that when he has his own battles and challenges going on, losing his mama and grandma close range at that. Raising his little brother and sister, and running a big clothing brand. When I'm silent, he gone fasho check in, and when he's silent, I do the same. We stay giving words of encouragement and uplifting each other. That's real, and I'll forever love and support Jay for that.

Ta'Rhonda Jones

My good sister from another mister, Ta'Rhonda Jones, I love her so much, and I'm so glad God placed her in my life. We'll be on the phone talking for hours, and she never rushes me off the phone. She'll listen to me vent and pray for me in the middle of it. Whenever I need her, she's there, no complaining. If she hasn't heard from me in three days to a week, she calls. She's a gift from God, and I am so thankful for all the words of encouragement and motivation she has given me. Her resilience and strength is unmatched. She lost her mom and still manages to show up for others; she is that listening ear and encourager, even when she probably isn't feeling her best. She told me something I'll never forget was to "Get out of God's way, bruh." And that's what I'm doing, getting out of God's way.

Jayla Lee

Jayla Lee, I know our bond and relationship came from God, because the way we connected was through Facebook Messenger, talking about a billboard and designs. Jayla and I have been locked in since. I can vent to her about whatever, whenever. We've been locked in for about two years now, and it feels like it's been 5+. She comes through for me with all my graphic designs (she's the best in the business), ideas, words of encouragement, and motivates me a lot with the many hats I wear. Jayla forever has my love and a place in my heart. She gives me strength as well, because losing a mother and a child, I know that's not easy at all, and she still manages to show up for a lot of people.

LaTonia Blankenship

LaTonia Blankenship, my big sister. Since the first day we met on a town hall panel, she's been a helping hand with everything I have going on and making sure I'm going in the right direction. She'll call me when I'm silent to check in on me and most definitely encourages me. Even when she has a lot that she's dealing with, she still manages to show up and support. When she's silent, I call her and drop some words of encouragement as well. The love I have for her can't be taken away.

To Whoever Needs This

To anybody that's reading and can relate to any of this, cut those people off. Just because y'all got history, that doesn't mean nothing. Some people come into your life for a reason and a season, and everybody is not meant to stay. That love you try to give everybody else who's abusing it, try giving that same love to yourself. You deserve it. Life isn't always beautiful, and life ain't easy, but you just can't give up. You got this. Keep fighting. This world is a better place with you in it. In order to grow, you gotta let go. Always remember that.

I Love You,

MQJ

CHAPTER SEVEN

The Work of Healing

Therapy, journaling, speaking, changing and hosting symposiums. Advocate born from survival.

CHAPTER SEVEN: The Work of Healing

Therapy, journaling, speaking, changing, and hosting symposiums. Advocate born from survival.

Therapy and the Turning Point

While on my healing journey, I was having sessions with my grief counselor, Dr. Sarita, once a week. What made me proud and motivated me to keep fighting and pushing through was when she told me that she saw a big difference in me compared to the first six months of 2022. I even felt different, new and whole, well, half whole, but I was better than ever. The journaling method she gave me helped along the way. I have about four journals full, and I still journal today. What I love about therapy is that it actually helps. What I realized is that going to therapy doesn't mean you're crazy, but not dealing with or talking about the things that's going on on the inside will most definitely make you crazy.

Choosing God and Therapy Over Medication

There were times I wanted to go to Lakeside (mental health clinic). I wanted to take meds to numb the pain I was feeling and escape the darkness and thoughts. But my God and therapy saved me and prevented me from going to a mental health clinic and taking meds. The doctors and meds do not have control over you or your mental health; God is in control. Just talk to Him, build a relationship with Him, and give therapy a try. But you also have to put in the work!

My First Time Speaking Out

December 2022, school guidance counselor Ms. Trina Freeman gave me my first public speaking opportunity at KIPP Middle School. I spoke at the students' Christmas program about grief, depression, holidays without loved ones, and I gave them some words of encouragement about grieving during the holidays and about not receiving much. Speaking at that school touched so many teachers and students, and it touched me deeply seeing how many people related to what I was speaking on. That's something that pushed me to go further with my advocacy work.

Telling My Story Publicly

February 2023, I filmed an episode of Express Yourself with Marlon, telling my mental health journey, and that was hard for me. It showed me that I was on the right track, but I still needed more healing. I brought my brother in on the episode to share some of his story. Some of the things I shared were my brother's first time hearing what I went through, and I still felt misunderstood, still felt alone. But I now know that when you're on a different journey than others, they won't understand you or hear you. Putting a lot of things out there publicly helped strengthen me as a person and helped me become more vulnerable.

Breaking the Silence

People told me I put too much personal stuff out there, that I shouldn't share this or that. I had to tell them, why would I sit on things that I have overcome that can help millions of people who are suffering in silence? That's the biggest problem, NOT talking about what we go through, just holding everything in. I'm not ashamed of anything that I went through because it made me stronger and built me into the person that I am today.

Healing Didn't Happen to Me

For a long time, I thought healing would be something that arrived like a blessing. Like a breakthrough moment where everything finally made sense, and the pain loosened its grip. But healing didn't just happen to me. I had to participate in it. I had to show up for it, even on days I didn't feel motivated, hopeful, or strong. There was no single prayer, conversation, or realization that fixed everything. Healing came in small, unglamorous steps. One therapy session. One honest journal entry. One boundary set with a shaking voice. One hard truth I stopped running from. Progress was measured in inches, not miles.

I Had to Get Honest

Healing required a level of honesty that felt terrifying at first. I had to admit that I wasn't okay. That I was tired. That I was angry. That I was hurting in ways I had minimized for years. I had to stop saying "I'm fine" when I wasn't, even to myself. You can't heal what you keep pretending doesn't exist. I wanted to be the strong one. The self-sufficient one. The one who figured it out quietly. But healing asked me to let people in, therapists, trusted friends, mentors, people who could hold space for my mess without trying to rush me out of it. Accepting help felt like weakness at first. It turned out to be courage.

I Had to Learn My Triggers

Part of the work was paying attention. What situations made my anxiety spike? What conversations left me spiraling? What environments drained me? Instead of judging myself for my reactions, I started getting curious about them. My triggers stopped being proof that I was broken and started becoming clues about what still needed care.

Boundaries Became Necessary

Healing meant I couldn't keep saying yes to everything and everyone. I had to disappoint people sometimes. I had to rest when others wanted more from me. I had to choose peace over people-pleasing. Boundaries weren't walls to keep love out; they were doors that helped me protect my energy so I could love without losing myself.

I Had to Sit With Feelings I Used to Avoid

Numbing had been my survival skill. Staying busy. Staying distracted. Staying productive. But healing asked me to sit still long enough to feel grief, fear, anger, and disappointment without running. That felt unbearable at first. But feelings, when felt safely, move. Avoided feelings stay stuck. Feelings slowly loosen.

Forgiving Took Work Too

Forgiveness wasn't instant, not for others, and definitely not for myself. I had to process the pain before I could release it. I had to acknowledge what hurt me without minimizing it. I had to accept that forgiving didn't mean something was okay; it meant I was choosing not to carry the weight forever.

My Habits Had to Change

Healing wasn't just emotional; it was practical. Sleep. Rest. What I consumed mentally and spiritually. How much I worked. How often I checked in with myself. I had to build routines that supported my well-being, not just my productivity. That meant discipline in areas I used to ignore.

I Had to Stop Romanticizing "Strong"

I used to think "Strong" meant pushing through, never slowing down, never needing help. Healing taught me a different kind of strength, the strength to cry, to cancel plans, to say "this is too much for me right now," to choose long-term health over short-term approval.

Progress Didn't Always Feel Good

Some breakthroughs came with tears, exhaustion, and temporary setbacks. Growth can feel like things are getting worse before they get better, because you're finally feeling what you once suppressed. I had to learn not to quit just because the work felt uncomfortable.

Healing Is Still Ongoing

The work didn't end when I started feeling better. It became maintenance. Check-ins. Adjustments. Grace on hard days. I still have to use the tools. I still have to be honest. I still have to rest. Healing isn't a destination I arrived at; it's a way I live now. Even on the hardest days, I can say this: the work of healing gave me my life back. Not a perfect life. Not a pain-free one. But a life where I feel more present, more aware, more in control of my choices instead of controlled by old wounds. The work was hard. But staying stuck was harder.

Mental Health Awareness and Advocacy

May 2023, Mental Health Awareness Month, I hosted two mental health symposiums, and both of them were a success. That was my first time hosting my own event. I set up an interview with FOX13 to promote and talk about my mental health symposiums, so the community could come and be a part of healing. Seeing the amount of people who needed that symposium motivated me even more, especially the black men. It was my family's first time hearing my story and knowing what I went through in 2022. Shout out to Jeremy Pierre and Stephanie Watkins at FOX13 for always coming through for me. Whenever I need an interview, they show up. Shout out to Gina Neely for always allowing me to come on her show, Bluff City Life with Gina Neely, to talk, share my mental health journey, and promote anything I had coming up. Last but not least, Alicia Renea ABC24, she supports me and my movement as well. She reached out to interview me on men's mental health and also came to see me speak. I'm thankful for them all.

Advocate Born From Survival

I'm a mental health advocate born from survival, born from pain, darkness, struggle, grief, a broken heart, and finding my way back with God. I'm advocating from experience, not research. When I advocate for mental health, I'm putting all of myself out there. I'm being the voice for all the ones who are suffering in silence, who feel alone, who feel misunderstood, who don't feel heard, and who think they're the only ones going through mental health challenges. No, I'm right here with y'all. I see y'all, I hear y'all, I understand y'all, and I love y'all. We're all gonna get through this. I couldn't just sit in silence after all that I've been through and overcome. I had to break my silence to help others and give them hope, because there is so much hope, man. I know I'm not the only one that wanted to end the pain and the voices, so that's why I had to tell my story.

CHAPTER EIGHT

Faith Over Feelings

Choosing to trust what God sees, even when
I don't understand what I'm living through.

CHAPTER EIGHT: Faith Over Feelings

Choosing to trust what God sees, even when I don't understand what I'm living through.

When Faith Feels Impossible

There are moments when faith feels impossible, when everything around me seems to fall apart, and I can't make sense of what God is doing or why He's doing it this way. Those are the moments that test me the most, not because I've lost faith, but because my feelings are louder than my trust. I've learned that faith isn't always about feeling strong. It's about believing that God is still working, even when I can't see the evidence. It's choosing to stand on what He said, not what my emotions say.

Questioning Everything

There were several seasons where I questioned everything, my purpose, my worth, my reason for living, even His presence. But every time I came to the end of myself, grace met me there. Quietly. Patiently. Faithfully. I remember one night when everything in me felt shattered. The weight of life, the silence of God, the ache in my chest, it all came crashing down at once. I sat in the dark asking the same question over and over: Why God? Why this? Why now? Why me? And for a long time, there was no answer, just stillness, pain, and my weed and liquor.

Peace in the Silence and Trusting Without Understanding

But somewhere in that silence, I felt a whisper, not in words, but in peace. It didn't explain anything, but it reminded me that I wasn't alone. Even in the chaos, He was still there. Still good. Still holding me together when I was falling apart. That's when I realized faith isn't about understanding; it's about trusting the One who already sees the outcome. My feelings told me I was forgotten, but my faith reminded me I was seen. My emotions said it was over, but my faith said, not yet.

Feelings Are Loud, But Feelings Aren't Facts

My feelings can be convincing. When anxiety rises, it doesn't politely knock; it barges in with evidence, worst-case scenarios, and a play-by-play of everything that could go wrong. When sadness shows up, it tells me it's always been this way and always will be. In those moments, my emotions don't feel temporary. They feel like the truth. I had to learn this slowly, and honestly, I still have to relearn it. Just because I feel forgotten doesn't mean I am. Just because I feel like a failure doesn't mean I've failed. Just because I feel alone doesn't mean I'm unsupported. Feelings are real, but they aren't always reliable narrators of what's actually happening in my life.

My Old Pattern

For a long time, my feelings made my decisions. If I felt afraid, I avoided. If I felt unworthy, I shrank. If I felt overwhelmed, I shut down. I thought I was being honest with myself, but really, I was letting temporary emotional weather determine the direction of my life.

Where Faith Steps In

Faith, for me, isn't pretending I don't have feelings. It's choosing not to let them drive. It's acknowledging the anxiety and still showing up. It's admitting I'm discouraged and still praying. It's saying, "I feel scared, but I'm going to take this step anyway because I believe I'm being guided, even if I can't see the full path yet."

Talking Back to My Thoughts

There are days I have to gently challenge my own mind. When the thought comes, You're not enough, faith answers, I am growing, and that's enough for today. When my mind says, You're alone in this, faith reminds me of the people who have shown up before, the ways I've been supported, the strength I didn't know I had until I needed it.

Faith Is Sometimes Repetition

I wish choosing faith was a one-time decision, but it's more like a daily practice. Sometimes hourly. I remind myself of what's true over and over again, especially when my emotions are loud. Not in a toxic positivity way, not by denying pain, but by refusing to let fear have the final word.

Jesus in the Storm, Not Just the Sun

I used to think faith worked best when life felt calm. Now I'm learning it's most real in the middle of emotional storms. Faith is what I hold onto when my feelings are spiraling, and

I don't trust my own perspective. It's the anchor when my inner world feels like waves.

Letting Feelings Sit, Not Steer

I don't shove my feelings down anymore. I let them be there. I name them. I feel them in my body. But I also picture them in the passenger seat, not the driver's seat. They get a voice, but they don't get the wheel. Faith is what helps me keep my hands steady in the direction I believe I'm meant to go.

Choosing Truth on Hard Days

Some days, faith looks small. It looks like getting out of bed when my feelings say stay hidden. It looks like sending the text, going to the appointment, taking the opportunity, or resting without guilt. It looks like whispering, God, I don't feel strong, but I trust You to be strong for me today.

Faith Over Feelings Doesn't Mean Ignoring Pain

This isn't about pretending everything is okay. It's about believing that how I feel in a moment isn't the full story of my life. My feelings matter, but they don't get to define my identity, my future, or my faith. They are part of my experience, not the authority over it.

What I'm Still Learning

I'm still learning the balance. Still learning when to sit with a feeling and when to speak truth over it. Still learning that faith isn't a personality trait, it's a choice I make again and again, especially when it would be easier to give in to fear.

The Quiet Strength of Faith

Faith over feelings is rarely dramatic. No music swelling. No instant transformation. Just quiet decisions, made in ordinary moments, that slowly build a life led by trust instead of fear. And over time, those small choices have changed me more than any single emotional high ever could.

Faith Doesn't Deny the Pain

Choosing faith over feelings doesn't mean pretending everything's okay. It means believing that God is still in control, even when it hurts. It's waking up each day and saying, "I don't get it, but I trust You anyway." Because faith doesn't erase the pain, it gives it purpose. Living faith over feelings isn't a one-time choice; it's a daily practice. There were mornings when I woke up still carrying the heaviness of yesterday, when anxiety whispered lies I almost believed. But each time, I made a conscious decision to pause and remind myself of the truth, that God sees what I cannot, knows what I cannot, and loves me even when I feel unlovable.

What Faith Looked Like for Me

For me, it looked like small acts: praying when I wanted to run, journaling when I wanted to hide, speaking out loud the promises I couldn't feel. It looked like trusting that each step forward, no matter how tiny, even when my emotions told me I was failing. Choosing faith over feelings meant leaning on God's perspective instead of my own, holding onto His promises when my heart was shaking.

CHAPTER NINE

When I Was Mad at God

Mad at God while still trusting and leaning on Him.

CHAPTER NINE: When I Was Mad at God

Mad at God while still trusting and leaning on Him.

I didn't stop believing in God.

I just stopped talking to Him.

There's a difference.

People imagine a crisis of faith as some dramatic moment, a lightning bolt, a slammed Bible, a declaration that you're done. Mine was quieter than that. Mine looked like staring at the ceiling at 2:17 a.m., eyes burning, heart pounding, whispering, "Why me? What have I done wrong?" into the dark like God was a roommate who'd left dirty dishes in the sink again.

I wasn't sad that night.

I was furious.

I had done everything I thought I was supposed to do. I tried to be kind. I tried to be strong. I tried to hold it together when my mind felt like it was unraveling thread by thread. I prayed when I didn't feel anything. I thanked God when I didn't understand what was happening. I told myself there was a plan.

But that night, the plan felt like a lie.

Something had broken in me, not all at once, but slowly, like a crack spreading across glass. My mental health had been slipping, and no matter how hard I tried to pray it away, journal it out, or "stay positive," I was sinking deeper into a version of myself I didn't recognize. My thoughts were louder than my faith. My fear was stronger than my hope.

And I was tired of pretending I was okay with it.

I remember thinking, If You're God, You see this. So why are you letting it happen?

That question felt dangerous. Disrespectful. Ungrateful. But it was also honest. And honesty has a way of clawing its way to the surface, no matter how spiritual you try to be.

I had grown up believing God was a protector, a comforter, a father. Someone who showed up. Someone who cared about the details. But when my mind became a place I didn't feel safe in, when getting out of bed felt like lifting a car off my chest, when I smiled in public and unraveled in private… God felt absent.

Or worse, indifferent.

I didn't want platitudes. I didn't want another "everything happens for a reason." I wanted relief. I wanted quiet in my head. I wanted to not feel like I was fighting a battle no one else could see. And the more I prayed without feeling any change, the more it felt like my words were hitting the ceiling and falling back down on me.

So I got mad.

Not the dramatic, shouting-at-the-sky kind of mad. The cold, tight, jaw-clenched kind. The kind where you stop reaching out because you don't want to be disappointed again.

I stopped praying the way I used to. No more polite check-ins. No more gratitude lists. When I did talk to God, it was sharp and short.

You could fix this.

You could help me.

You're not, though.

And then came the guilt.

Because who gets mad at God and expects life to go well after that? I worried I was making everything worse. Maybe my mental health was struggling because I wasn't faithful enough. Maybe I was being taught a lesson. Maybe this was punishment.

That thought burrowed deep.

I started to see my pain as proof of failure. If I were stronger, I wouldn't be struggling like this. If I trusted God more, I wouldn't feel so anxious. If I were more grateful, I wouldn't feel so empty.

So now I wasn't just drowning in my own mind, I was ashamed of drowning.

I didn't tell many people about that part. It's easier to say "I was going through a hard time" than "I thought God had abandoned me and maybe it was my fault." That kind of honesty feels risky, especially in communities where faith is supposed to look unshakable.

But the truth is, my anger at God was tangled up with my mental health. I wasn't just questioning Him, I was questioning my worth, my strength, my place in the world. If God felt distant, then I felt alone. And when you already feel alone inside your own head, that distance can feel unbearable.

There were days I'd sit in silence, not praying, not reading anything inspirational, just existing in this heavy, numb space. Drinking and smoking. I told myself I was taking a "break," but really, I was grieving. Grieving the version of faith I used to have. Grieving the version of myself that felt more certain, more hopeful, more okay.

Anger was easier to hold than sadness.

Anger made me feel powerful, at least for a moment. Sadness made me feel small.

But underneath every frustrated thought I had toward God was a quieter one I didn't want to admit:

I still wanted Him to be there.

That was the part that confused me. If I was so mad, why did I still feel disappointed? Why did I still wish things were different? Why did I still, in my lowest moments, almost whisper a prayer before catching myself?

Because anger doesn't always mean you've stopped caring.

Sometimes it means you care so much that the pain has nowhere else to go.

Looking back, I can see I wasn't just mad at God. I was mad at feeling helpless. Mad at my own mind for turning against me. Mad that I couldn't fix it by being disciplined or faithful or positive enough. God became the safest place to put that anger, big enough to hold it, silent enough not to argue back.

I didn't know it then, but that anger was still a form of relationship. A strained one. A quiet one. But not an absent one.

I thought faith meant never questioning, never doubting, never feeling disappointed. But that season taught me something different: sometimes faith looks like staying in the conversation, even when the only words you have are, "I don't understand," and "This hurts," and "Where are You?"

I was mad at God.

But I was still talking to Him.

And that, even in my anger, meant the story wasn't over.

People don't talk enough about being mad at God. We talk about trusting Him, praising Him, leaning on Him, but nobody really talks about the anger. The kind of anger that sits in your chest when you've prayed, believed, waited, and still ended up hurting. I wasn't mad because I didn't believe in God. I was mad because I did.

I was mad because I trusted Him. Because I called on Him in the darkest moments of my life and still felt like He was silent. I was mad because I kept asking, Why me? And the answers never came. I watched other people live freely while I felt like I was barely surviving. And it felt unfair. It felt like God was asking too much of me when I was already carrying more than I could handle.

There were nights I talked to God without a filter. No church voice. No pretty prayers. Just real, raw words, even curse words at times. No lie, I'm being honest. I questioned His timing, His silence, and His plan. I asked Him why He would allow so much pain in my life when all I was trying to do was hold on. I told Him I didn't understand why He would take people I loved and leave me here to grieve the loss alone.

What hurt the most wasn't just the pain; it was the confusion. I didn't understand how God could be good and still let me hurt this badly. I didn't understand how I could be faithful and still feel forgotten. I wrestled with the thought that maybe God was disappointed in me, or maybe I wasn't praying hard enough, or maybe I was being punished.

But even in my anger, I never walked away. I complained. I questioned. I cried. But I stayed. And that's when I realized something important: staying angry with God is still staying connected to God. I learned that He wasn't offended by my honesty. He wasn't distant because I was mad. He was right there, letting me feel what I needed to feel instead of forcing me to fake faith.

Slowly, my anger turned into surrender. Not because everything made sense, but because I realized God never left me in my pain. He sat with me in it. He held me when I couldn't hold myself. And even when I didn't understand Him, He still understood me.

CHAPTER TEN

What's Still Hard

Even when you're healing, things are still hard.

CHAPTER TEN: What's Still Hard

Even when you're healing, things are still hard.

I wish I could tell you everything got easier.

Once I started working on my mental health, rebuilt my faith, and learned the language for what I was going through, the hard parts just… faded. That I wake up every day grounded and unshaken. That I never spiral. That I never doubt. That I never have to fight my own mind.

I wish healing worked like that.

But some things are still hard.

Not in the dramatic, rock-bottom way they once were. Not in the "I don't know how I'm going to survive this" way. It's quieter now. More subtle. But it's there. Like background noise you can ignore most days, until you suddenly can't.

Some mornings, my first thought is still heavy.

There's no clear reason. Nothing terrible has happened. My life, on paper, looks full and meaningful. I have a purpose. I have people who love me. I have tools now, coping skills, language and awareness. And yet, every now and then, I wake up with that familiar weight in my chest, like my body remembered a sadness my mind hasn't caught up to yet.

That's still hard.

I still have days when my thoughts turn on me faster than I expect. One small mistake, one awkward interaction, one moment of feeling misunderstood, and suddenly my brain is building a case against me. You're not doing enough. You're disappointing people. You should be better by now.

The difference is, now I notice it happening.

Before, I believed every thought. Now, I argue back. I take a breath. I ask, is this true, or is this fear talking? Growth hasn't silenced the voice; it just taught me not to hand it the microphone.

But it's still tiring to have that conversation in your head.

Faith is still hard sometimes, too.

I don't feel as angry at God as I once did, but I don't feel constantly certain either. There are still prayers that feel like they float into space. Still moments when I wonder why some wounds take so long to heal. Still situations where I catch myself thinking, I thought we worked through this already.

I've learned that faith isn't a straight line. It's a relationship. And like any relationship, there are close seasons and quiet ones. There are days I feel deeply held, and days I feel like I'm walking on my own, hoping I'm still being guided even when I can't feel it.

Trusting without constant reassurance?

That's still hard.

I also still struggle with the instinct to perform wellness.

When you become "the strong one" or "the inspiring one" or "the person who made it through," people stop expecting you to have bad days. They come to you for hope. For strength. For perspective. And I'm honored by that, I truly am.

But sometimes I want to say, I'm still in this, too.

Sometimes I leave a room where I encouraged everyone else and sit alone with feelings I didn't get to share. Sometimes I remind people they're allowed to not be okay, while quietly wondering if I'm allowed to say the same thing out loud.

Letting people see the unfinished parts of me?

Still hard.

Rest is still hard.

There's a part of me that believes if I slow down, everything will fall apart. That my worth is tied to what I produce, how much I give and how well I hold everything together. Even after everything I've learned, I still have to consciously tell myself that existing is enough. That I don't have to earn my right to breathe by being useful.

Some days I believe that.

Some days I'm still trying to.

And then there's forgiveness, of myself.

I can extend grace to almost anyone else. I understand trauma. I understand mental health. I understand coping mechanisms and survival responses, and how people do the best they can with what they have.

But when it comes to my own past? The times I shut down. The times I pushed people away. The ways my pain leaked onto others before I knew how to manage it?

That's still hard to look at with softness.

Healing has helped me take responsibility without drowning in shame. But shame still knocks sometimes. It still tries to tell me I should have known better, done better, been better, even when I was just trying to survive.

I'm learning to answer it with compassion instead of punishment.

Learning. Not mastered.

That's the theme, really.

I am healthier than I was. More aware. More grounded. More honest. I have more peace than chaos now. More tools than panic. More connection than isolation.

But healing didn't turn me into someone who never struggles.

It turned me into someone who knows how to stay when things get hard. Someone who can feel a wave of sadness without assuming it will drown me. Someone who can question a thought instead of becoming it. Someone who can say, Today is hard, without believing, My life is hopeless.

What's still hard doesn't erase how far I've come.

It just reminds me that growth is ongoing. That being human doesn't end when healing begins. That strength isn't the absence of struggle; it's the willingness to keep showing up inside your own life, even when old feelings revisit like uninvited guests.

Some things are still hard.

But I'm not as afraid of hard as I used to be.

And that, in itself, is healing.

Healing didn't erase everything, and I don't say that lightly. There are still mornings when I wake up and feel tired before the day even starts. Not physically tired, but soul tired. The kind of tiredness that comes from carrying a lot of life for a long time. Some days I feel strong and grounded, and other days it feels like I'm holding myself together with quiet prayers and deep breaths.

What's still hard is realizing that some things don't get better, they just get different. The grief doesn't disappear; it changes shape. I don't cry the same way I used to, but the ache is still there. It lives on certain dates, certain places, certain moments when I wish I could pick up the phone and call someone who's no longer here. I've learned how to live with the loss, but that doesn't mean it doesn't still hurt.

What's still hard is accepting that not everyone will understand who I've become. Some people only knew me in survival mode, and they don't recognize me in healing. Growth can make people uncomfortable, especially when they benefited from the old version of you. Letting go of those connections was painful, but holding onto them would've cost me more.

What's still hard is learning to slow down. For so long, being busy felt safe. Stillness gave my thoughts room to talk, and sometimes those thoughts weren't kind. I'm still learning that rest isn't a weakness and that peace doesn't mean something bad is about to happen. My body is still unlearning years of survival.

What's still hard is loving deeply after being hurt deeply. Even now, there are moments when I pull back out of instinct, not intention. I want connection, but I also remember the pain of trusting people who couldn't meet me where I was. Healing hasn't removed that memory; it's just teaching me how to move forward with wisdom instead of fear.

CHAPTER ELEVEN

What I'm Still Trusting God For

When I've seen God's hand and have no choice
but to trust Him.

CHAPTER ELEVEN: What I'm Still Trusting God For

When I've seen God's hand and have no choice but to trust Him.

I used to think faith was about being sure.

Sure God would come through.

Sure things would make sense.

Sure the prayers would be answered the way I hoped.

Now I think faith is often just choosing not to walk away when you don't have proof yet.

There are still things in my life that don't have neat endings. Still, prayers that feel mid-sentence. Still areas where I'm doing the work, showing up, healing… and waiting.

Waiting is hard for me.

I like the growth I can measure. Progress I can point to. Results that make the struggle feel worth it. But some of the most important things I'm trusting God for right now don't come with timelines or tracking numbers.

I'm still trusting God with my mind.

I've learned tools. I've done the therapy. I've had breakthroughs. But mental health isn't a one-time fix; it's maintenance, awareness, and grace over and over again. I still have days where old thoughts knock on the door. Days when I have to actively choose truth over fear. Days when I have to rest more than I planned because my nervous system is tired.

I'm trusting that healing will continue, even when it's slow.

Those setbacks don't erase progress. That God isn't disappointed in the pace of my growth.

I'm still trusting God with my purpose.

There are dreams in my heart that haven't fully unfolded yet. Things I feel called to do that feel bigger than my current capacity. Impact I hope to have. Lives I hope to reach. Stories I hope to tell.

Sometimes I feel confident about it. Other times, I wonder if I missed a step, if I'm behind, if I'm enough to carry what I feel called to.

Trust, for me, looks like continuing to prepare even when the full picture isn't visible. It looks like saying yes to small steps while the big vision is still blurry. It looks like believing that what's meant for me doesn't require me to destroy myself to get there.

I'm still trusting God with my relationships.

Healing changed how I show up with people. I have stronger boundaries now. More honesty. More awareness of what I need and what I can give. But that also means some relationships have shifted. Some ended. Some are still being rebuilt in healthier ways.

It's vulnerable to let people see the real you, not the high-functioning, "I've got it" version, but the one who still has tender spots. I'm trusting God to bring and keep people in my life who can hold both my strength and my softness. People who don't just celebrate what I do, but care about who I am when I'm tired, quiet, or unsure.

I'm also trusting Him with the loneliness that sometimes comes with growth. Outgrowing old dynamics can feel like standing in between chapters, not where you were, not fully where you're going.

That in-between space requires trust.

I'm still trusting God with the parts of my story that don't make sense yet.

There are things I've walked through that I understand now. I can see how they shaped me, deepened me and prepared me. But there are other parts I still don't have answers for. Prayers that were answered differently than I wanted. Doors that closed without explanation. Pain that didn't come with a clear lesson attached.

I don't always get it.

But I'm learning that trust doesn't always come from understanding; sometimes it comes from remembering. Remembering the times I thought I wouldn't make it and did. The seasons I thought would break me and instead built resilience I didn't know I had. The ways provision, support, and strength showed up, even if not in the forms I expected.

My faith now is less about certainty and more about history.

I've been carried before.

I've been held together before.

I've been guided before.

So even when I can't see clearly, I'm choosing to believe I'm not walking alone now.

Even after all God has done in my life, there are still moments and seasons I'm waiting on Him to move. I've experienced His goodness in ways I never could have imagined, yet there are areas of my heart, my dreams, and my life that still feel unfinished. Some of these things have been with me for years, others only for months, but the truth is, I'm still learning what it means to trust God when I can't see the whole picture.

I'm still trusting God for clarity when I feel lost. There are decisions I've wrestled with, roads I've wondered if I should take, and directions that don't make sense yet. Some days I long for a sign, a word, a clear answer, but instead, I'm learning to step forward in faith, even when the way is uncertain.

I'm still trusting God with the things I don't have control over. The parts of my life that feel unfinished. The prayers that haven't been answered yet. The doors that didn't open when I thought they would. Trusting God now looks like surrendering outcomes, not just asking for them.

I'm still trusting God with my future. There was a time I needed to know every step, every plan, every detail. Now, I've learned that clarity isn't always immediate. Sometimes God reveals things in pieces, and I have to be faithful with what's in front of me instead of stressing over what's next.

I'm trusting God with my calling. With the responsibility that comes with being visible and vulnerable. I pray often that

I never speak from a place of ego or performance. I want to be led, not loud. I want to help without harming myself in the process.

I'm still trusting God with my healing. Healing in my heart, in relationships, in areas of my life that feel broken. Sometimes the wounds are visible, sometimes they're hidden, but either way, I know God's power is greater than the pain I carry. And even when it feels like the scars will never fade, I hold onto His promise to restore. There are parts of me that are better and parts of me that are still tender. I trust that God knows the difference. I trust that He's patient with me on days I feel behind. I trust that He's not rushing my process, even when I feel like I should be further along.

I'm trusting God to keep my heart soft in a world that hardens people. To keep me honest, humble, and grounded. Trusting God now isn't dramatic; it's consistent. It's choosing Him daily, even when my faith feels quiet.

I'm still trusting God for provision. Not just financially, though that matters, but provision in life, opportunities, purpose, peace, and connection. There have been seasons of waiting, seasons of watching doors close, and seasons where I questioned if I'd ever see a breakthrough. Yet, I'm learning that God's timing is perfect, even when it's hard to understand.

I'm still trusting God for patience. Patience when the waiting is long, when the answer feels delayed, when I want to rush the process. Trusting God doesn't mean I'm never frustrated or tired; it means I choose to believe that He is working behind the scenes, even when I can't feel it.

And maybe the hardest thing I'm trusting God for is trust itself. To keep believing when the evidence feels small. To keep walking forward when I don't see the finish line. To keep surrendering my expectations, my timeline, and my understanding, knowing that His ways are higher than mine.

Some days I want to scream at heaven. Other days, I whisper, quietly, "I trust You, God," even when I don't feel it. And somehow, in that tension, faith grows. Hope blooms. And I remember that trusting God isn't about having the answer today, it's about holding onto Him through the unknown, trusting that He is good and that His plans are perfect.

Trusting God doesn't mean I never worry. It doesn't mean I never have questions. It doesn't mean I don't feel the weight of the unknown sometimes.

It means when fear gets loud, I don't let it make all my decisions.

It means I keep praying, even if the prayers are simple.

Help me. Guide me. Give me strength for today.

It means I release the illusion that I can control every outcome and instead focus on being faithful with what's in front of me right now: my healing, my work, my relationships, my honesty.

There's still so much I'm waiting on.

Still growth I want to see.

Still peace I'm learning to hold onto.

Still parts of me that are becoming.

But I'm no longer trusting God the way I did before, with blind optimism and unspoken fear of disappointment.

I'm trusting Him with open eyes now. With the knowledge that life can be hard, that I can struggle, that answers don't always come quickly.

And still, I'm choosing to trust. Not because everything is resolved.

But because I've learned I don't have to have everything figured out to keep taking the next step.

So today, I choose to keep trusting. For healing, for clarity, for provision, for patience, for faith itself. I don't know when the answers will come, or what the full picture looks like, but I know the One I'm trusting. And that is enough.

CHAPTER TWELVE

What Success Didn't Heal

Success doesn't heal pain or trauma.

CHAPTER TWELVE: What Success Didn't Heal

Success doesn't heal pain or trauma.

From the outside, it looked like everything was working.

Opportunities were coming. Doors were opening. I was accomplishing things I once prayed for. The kind of milestones people celebrate. The kind of moments that make great announcements, great captions and great applause.

And I was grateful. I truly was.

But behind the scenes, there were nights I still felt empty in rooms full of praise.

No one really talks about that part.

We're taught to believe success is the cure. That once you "make it," whatever it is for you, the insecurities quiet down, the sadness lifts, and the self-doubt disappears. That achievement and healing arrive hand in hand.

They don't.

Success changed my circumstances.

It didn't automatically change my inner world.

I still had the same mind. The same thought patterns. The same old wounds that didn't magically close just because my résumé looked better.

There were moments I walked off stages, left meetings, finished projects I once dreamed about… and instead of feeling full, I felt strangely numb. Like I had reached the destination and realized I had brought all my unhealed parts with me.

Because success doesn't evict pain. It just gives it better lighting.

I thought if I could just get busy enough, productive enough, visible enough, I'd outrun the parts of me that felt small. I told myself I was "focused" and "driven." And I was. But if I'm honest, I was also avoiding stillness, because stillness meant being alone with thoughts I didn't know how to soothe yet.

Achievement became a distraction that looked like purpose.

And the world claps for that.

The praise felt good, but it was temporary. Applause fades fast when you're lying awake at night questioning your worth in silence. Compliments don't stick when your inner voice is louder and harsher. Accomplishments don't automatically rewrite the stories you learned about yourself when you were hurting.

I could be celebrated publicly and still criticize myself privately.

That disconnect was confusing.

I remember thinking, Why am I still struggling? Look at everything I have. Look at how far I've come. Then came the guilt. Because how dare I feel anxious, overwhelmed, or low when my life looked "blessed"? How dare I have hard days when other people would trade places with me in a second?

So I smiled. I performed gratitude. I told myself to be thankful and push through.

But gratitude and grief can exist in the same body.

I was thankful for the opportunities and still tired in my soul. Proud of what I was building and still unsure of who I was without the work. Surrounded by people and still lonely in ways I couldn't explain.

Success amplified something I didn't expect: pressure.

Pressure to maintain it.

Pressure to deserve it.

Pressure to not mess it up.

Every win quietly whispered, Don't lose this. And fear is a heavy thing to carry while you're trying to heal.

There were days I tied my worth to my productivity so tightly that resting felt like failure. If I wasn't creating, achieving, moving forward, I felt like I was falling behind, not just in my career, but as a person.

No amount of external validation fixed that.

Because the voice telling me I wasn't enough didn't come from the outside. It lived inside me, long before any success showed up.

I had to learn that healing is internal work. Slow work. Quiet work. The kind no one claps for. The kind that doesn't trend or get announced. The kind that happens in therapy sessions, honest conversations, tearful prayers, and journal pages no one else will ever read.

Success gave me platforms.

Healing gave me peace, and only when I actually did the work.

I also had to face the uncomfortable truth that I sometimes used success to avoid vulnerability. It's easier to show people what you're building than to show them where you're breaking. Easier to talk about projects than pain. Easier to stay busy than to admit you're not okay.

But eventually, the pace catches up with you.

Your body starts asking for rest.

Your mind starts asking for care.

Your soul starts asking for honesty.

And no achievement can answer those requests for you.

I'm still proud of what I've accomplished. That pride is real. The gratitude is real. The joy is real.

But now I know those things can exist alongside the need for therapy. Alongside hard days. Alongside moments of doubt. Alongside a healing journey that doesn't end just because the outside of my life looks good.

Success didn't heal my anxiety.

It didn't erase my past.

It didn't automatically teach me how to love myself.

It just gave me a bigger stage to realize I still needed to.

What healed me, and is still healing me, is learning that my worth was never supposed to be built on applause. That I am allowed to be a work in progress, even while I'm winning. That I can celebrate my growth without pretending I've arrived.

Success changed my life.

But healing changed me.

Success didn't heal my trauma. It didn't stop the flashbacks, the triggers, or the emotional waves that come without warning. No award, recognition, or opportunity could undo what my nervous system had already learned.

Success didn't heal my grief. It didn't bring anyone back. It didn't sit with me in my hardest moments. I learned quickly that success is loud, but grief is quiet, and the quiet always speaks louder when you're alone.

There were moments I reached goals I once prayed for and still felt empty afterward. That was hard to admit. I thought success would feel like relief. Instead, it exposed what still needed healing. It showed me that external wins can't fix internal wounds.

Success didn't replace therapy. It didn't replace self-reflection. It didn't replace God. I still had to do the work, sit with uncomfortable truths, face my pain, and learn healthier ways to cope.

Success opened doors, but it didn't close emotional wounds. Once I stopped expecting it to save me, I could finally enjoy it without pressure. Success became something I experienced, not something I leaned on.

I used to think success would fix everything. I thought if I achieved enough, if I earned enough, performed enough, got recognition, or reached the milestones I'd set for myself, then all the pain, all the doubts, all the loneliness inside me would disappear.

But it didn't.

Success brought applause, but it didn't bring peace. It brought opportunities, but it didn't bring purpose. It brought validation from the world, but it didn't quiet the voice inside that whispered, "You're not enough."

I've accomplished things I'm proud of. I've stood on stages, received awards, launched projects, and hit goals I once thought were impossible. And yet, in the quiet moments, in the spaces between the lights and the accolades, the old wounds were still there. The fear, the anxiety, the insecurities, they didn't vanish just because I achieved something external.

I realized that success is like a spotlight: it illuminates the surface but doesn't reach the deep places of the heart. No amount of recognition, praise, or material gain could fill the emptiness I was carrying. No applause could erase past pain or rewrite the stories I'd told myself about who I was.

What success didn't heal, God did.

It was only in surrender, in prayer, and in learning to lean on Him that I began to understand that worth isn't measured by achievements, followers, or titles. Healing doesn't come from climbing a ladder; it comes from allowing God to meet you where you are, with all your scars, all your doubts, all your "not enoughs."

I had to learn that I could celebrate victories without expecting them to fix me. That I could pursue excellence without letting it define my identity. That the validation I craved from the world was nothing compared to the affirmation I find in God's love.

Success taught me many things; it taught me discipline, creativity, courage, and perseverance. But what it didn't teach me, what it couldn't heal, was me. That part only God could reach. And slowly, I began to let Him do it. Slowly, I began to let myself be made whole, not by what I achieved, but by who I am.

CHAPTER THIRTEEN

What Peace Actually Feels Like Now

Peace after the years of darkness, pain and trauma.

CHAPTER THIRTEEN: What Peace Actually Feels Like Now

Peace after the years of darkness, pain and trauma.

I used to chase peace like it was something I could earn or find in the right place, the right people, or the right circumstances. I thought it lived in perfect control, in the absence of chaos, in the "all-clear" moments of life. But I was wrong.

Peace isn't the absence of trouble. It's not a life without storms. It's not even always quiet; it's something deeper, something steadier, something that holds you even when everything else shakes.

Now, peace feels like a deep, quiet confidence that God is still God. It's the calm in the middle of uncertainty, the gentle whisper that says, "I am with you, and I am enough." It's the freedom to breathe without fear, the courage to keep moving even when the path is unclear, and the surrender that comes from knowing I don't have to carry it all alone.

Peace feels like letting go of what I can't control. It's releasing expectations of people, outcomes, and timing, and resting in the truth that God's timing is perfect, even when mine isn't. It's the ability to sit in a moment without rushing, to savor a sunset, a conversation, a laugh, without needing it to fix me or define me.

Peace feels like forgiveness, of myself, of others, of the things that hurt me. It's not a single act, but a daily choice: to release bitterness, resentment, and regret. To exchange worry for trust. To trade fear for faith.

Peace feels like presence. Not just being present with God, but being present with myself, honoring my feelings, acknowledging my pain, and letting my heart rest in a love that never fails. It's quiet, steady, and sometimes so subtle that I almost miss it, but it's always there, like a river running beneath the surface of my life.

Peace now feels quieter than I imagined it would. It's not constant happiness or excitement. It's stable. It's not waking up in fight-or-flight every day. It's being able to breathe without bracing for impact.

Peace feels like emotional safety. Feeling my emotions without being consumed by them. Letting myself cry without falling apart. Being triggered and still choosing a healthier response.

Peace feels like discernment. Knowing when to speak and when to stay silent. Knowing who deserves access to me and who doesn't. Peace has taught me that not every battle needs my energy.

Peace feels like trusting myself again. Trusting my instincts. Trusting my growth. Trusting that I can handle whatever comes next because I've already survived so much.

Peace doesn't mean life is easy. It means life no longer controls me the way it used to. Peace feels like coming home to myself. Like finally being okay with where I am, while still believing there's more ahead.

Peace feels like hope that doesn't depend on circumstances. It's a gentle confidence that no matter what comes, I am seen, I am held, I am loved. And that's enough.

CHAPTER FOURTEEN

What Healing Looks Like Today

What healing looks like after all that I have overcome.

CHAPTER FOURTEEN: What Healing Looks Like Today

What healing looks like after all that I have overcome.

Healing today doesn't look like perfection. It doesn't look like I never have hard days or heavy thoughts. It looks like awareness. It looks like honesty. It looks like choosing myself in ways I never knew how to before.

Healing isn't a single moment. It's not a checkbox you mark and move on. It's not a perfect, polished version of yourself that appears overnight. Healing, I've learned, is messy, slow, and often invisible to the outside world.

I still have moments when grief shows up unannounced. Certain dates, certain smells, certain songs can take me right back. The difference now is I don't run from it. I sit with it. I let myself feel without judgment, without shame. I've learned that healing isn't about avoiding pain; it's about learning how to carry it without letting it carry me.

Healing looks like boundaries. Saying no without explaining myself, saying no when I used to say yes out of fear or obligation. Walking away without guilt. It looks like protecting my energy, my mind, and my heart, even when others don't understand. Healing means knowing my worth isn't tied to anyone else's approval. Protecting my peace even when it disappoints people. I used to feel bad for choosing distance, but now I understand that not everyone is meant to walk with me in every season. Some people were part of my survival, not my future.

Healing looks like forgiveness, not because the other person deserves it, but because I deserve peace. It looks like letting go of resentment, of grudges, of old stories that no longer serve me. Healing is realizing that carrying anger only weighs me down and choosing freedom instead.

Healing looks like self-compassion. It looks like speaking to myself with gentleness instead of criticism. It looks like showing up for myself in ways I used to only show up for others. Healing is understanding that I am allowed to rest, to stumble, and to grow at my own pace.

Healing looks like faith that keeps moving forward, even when the pain lingers. It's trusting God in the cracks, in the scars, and in the unfinished parts of my story. It's recognizing that restoration isn't about perfection, it's about progress, resilience, and God's gentle work in me over time.

Healing looks like freedom. Freedom to feel, to cry, to laugh, to hope. Freedom to be fully human without shame or guilt. It's quiet victories, small joys, and the moments when I realize I'm no longer defined by what hurt me, but by who I'm becoming in the process.

Healing looks like consistency. Praying even when I don't feel spiritual. Journaling when my thoughts get loud. Checking in with myself instead of waiting for a breakdown to remind me that something's wrong. It's not dramatic, it's daily.

Healing looks like taking responsibility for my mental health without blaming myself for what I went through. I stopped asking, "What's wrong with me?" and started asking,

"What happened to me?" That shift changed everything. It gave me compassion for myself instead of criticism.

Healing looks like trusting God without rushing Him. I no longer demand answers on my timeline. I've learned to rest in the process, even when it's uncomfortable. Faith now feels steadier, not loud, not forced, just present.

Healing looks like showing up for others without losing myself. I help from a full place, not an empty one. I pour without draining. I give without disappearing. I've learned that I can be supportive without being self-destructive.

Healing looks like joy without guilt. Laughing again. Dreaming again. Wanting more out of life without feeling like I'm betraying my pain or my past. I finally understand that surviving something doesn't mean I owe my suffering the rest of my life.

Healing looks like grace. On the days I fall short. On the days I get tired. On the days I don't have the words. I don't beat myself up anymore. I remind myself how far I've come.

Healing today looks like peace, not the absence of struggle, but the presence of God in the middle of it. I'm not who I used to be, and I'm not finished becoming who I'm meant to be. And for the first time, I'm okay with that.

CHAPTER FIFTEEN

Things I Wanted to Say But Couldn't

Things that were on my mind and heart but didn't know how to say them.

CHAPTER FIFTEEN: Things I Wanted to Say But Couldn't

Things that were on my mind and heart but didn't know how to say them.

There are so many things I wanted to say, but couldn't. Things that stayed trapped in my chest because I wasn't ready, because the timing wasn't right, because people wouldn't understand, or maybe because I didn't understand myself yet.

I wanted to tell my grandma how much her love shaped me. How her words still echo in my mind. How I still reach for her in moments of doubt, needing guidance I can't find anywhere else. I wanted to tell her that I carry her in me, every decision I make, every prayer I say, every time I try to be a better person. I wanted to tell her that losing her broke me, but somehow also taught me resilience I didn't know I had. I couldn't. She wasn't here to hear it, and that hurt.

I wanted to say, *I'm not okay,*

but I had already convinced everyone, including myself, that I was "just tired."

I wanted to say, *I'm drowning,*

but you kept complimenting how well I was swimming.

I wanted to say, *that hurt,*

but I didn't have proof, only a feeling, and I didn't trust my feelings yet.

I wanted to say, *please don't joke about that,*

but I was the "strong one," and strong people aren't supposed to be sensitive.

I wanted to say, *I need help,*

but I thought needing help meant I had failed some invisible test everyone else had passed.

I wanted to say, *I'm scared of my own thoughts,*

but I didn't have language for something I was trying so hard not to admit was real.

I wanted to say, *I can't keep carrying this,*

but I didn't know who I could safely set it down with.

I wanted to say, *I'm trying,*

on the days it looked like I was distant, irritable, or checked out.

I wasn't giving up. I was surviving in quiet ways no one could see.

I wanted to say, *your words stayed with me,*

the sharp ones, the dismissive ones, the "you're overreacting" ones, but I didn't want to seem dramatic, so I swallowed them and let them echo instead.

I wanted to say, *I needed you then,*

not when I got better, not when I was easier to be around,

but when I was inconvenient, messy, and hard to understand.

I wanted to say, *I didn't choose this,*

as if anyone would wake up and pick anxiety, depression, numbness, shame, as if this was a personality flaw and not a nervous system waving a white flag.

I wanted to tell people how much their absence felt when I needed them most. How their words, or their silence, left scars I couldn't explain. How I was there for them when they cried, when they needed someone to lean on, but when I cried, I felt like the world turned away. I wanted to scream that out. I wanted to cry it out. But sometimes saying it felt selfish, or worse, futile, so I swallowed it instead.

I wanted to tell God I was angry. That I was mad, frustrated, and lost. I didn't understand why I had to endure so much pain. I wanted to ask Him why the nights were so long, why grief hit so hard, why the silence felt deafening. I wanted to shout, cry or even curse. I wanted to let it all out. But I didn't know if it was okay to be honest in my anger with Him, so I stayed quiet for a long time, wrestling with faith in private. Until I couldn't stay quiet anymore.

I wanted to tell the version of me that almost gave up that I see them now. That I survived. That the tears, the fear, the sleepless nights didn't win. I wanted to tell myself that staying alive was the bravest thing they could do, even when it didn't feel like bravery at all. I wanted to say, "You did it. You made it through." But for so long, I couldn't even speak to that version of me without remembering how broken I was.

I wanted to say, *I forgive you,*

and sometimes I did, silently, alone, because holding the anger was heavier than releasing it.

But mostly, I wanted to say, *I forgive myself.*

For not speaking sooner.

For not knowing how.

For coping in ways that made sense at the time, even if they don't make sense now.

For staying when I should've left, and leaving when I didn't understand why.

These were the words I buried to survive.

And maybe I couldn't say them then, because back then, I was still learning that my voice was allowed to take up space.

Now, I'm not whispering them anymore.

Now, I'm saying them out loud, not to blame, not to reopen wounds, but to finally let the silence go.

I want to tell the people reading this, especially those grieving, broken, or suicidal, that they are not alone. That I've been there. That I understand the weight of the nights when nothing makes sense. That it's okay to hurt, it's okay to cry, it's okay to feel lost, but it's not okay to give up. I want to tell them I see them, I hear them, and I love them. I still want to say that, every day, as loud as I can.

Some of these things I still haven't said out loud. Some of them I whisper in my journal or in prayers. Some of them I speak through my advocacy, through my work, through my art, through my story. And maybe that's enough. Maybe saying it in pieces, in moments, in action, is how it's meant to be shared.

The weight of things left unsaid can feel heavy, but it also reminds me that I survived long enough to have a voice. I have a story worth telling. That even if I couldn't say it then, I can say it now. And maybe, by saying it now, I'm speaking for all the versions of myself that didn't have the courage, or the space, to speak.

CHAPTER SIXTEEN

When Advocacy Felt Heavy Instead of Healing

Thinking mental health advocacy was healing at one point.

CHAPTER SIXTEEN: When Advocacy Felt Heavy Instead of Healing

Thinking mental health advocacy was healing at one point.

At first, telling my story felt like exhaling after holding my breath for years.

Every time I spoke, something loosened. Shame had less power. Silence had less control. I felt like I was turning pain into purpose, like the hard parts of my life were finally for something.

Advocacy felt like healing out loud.

Until one day, it didn't.

Somewhere along the way, my story stopped being something I shared and started being something people expected.

I wasn't just a person anymore,

I was a testimony.

A survival arc.

An inspirational before-and-after.

People thanked me for my vulnerability, but I went home feeling exposed in a way I couldn't name. Every panel, every interview, every message that started with "you have a powerful story that will save many lives…"

was beautiful and heavy at the same time.

Because I was still living it.

I was still having hard mornings. Still managing my mind. Still human. But advocacy made it feel like I had to be the finished version of myself. The healed one. The hopeful one. The strong one. There were days I needed support, but I felt like I had accidentally signed a contract to always be the one giving it.

I started measuring my bad days against the people who told me I inspired them. I started feeling guilty for struggling. I started wondering if I was allowed to fall apart when "so many people were counting on me."

That's when I knew the weight had shifted.

Advocacy is powerful, but it's not meant to replace your own healing. It's not meant to turn your wounds into a public utility. I had to learn that I'm allowed to have a private life.

That isn't a lesson.

A pain that isn't packaged.

A breakdown that doesn't become a caption.

I had to relearn that I am a person first,

and a voice second.

That saying "not today" doesn't make me a fraud. That protecting my peace doesn't betray my purpose. That I can care deeply about others without offering myself up as proof of survival every single time.

Advocacy stopped feeling heavy

when I stopped carrying it alone.

When I let other voices speak. When I let myself rest. When I remembered that the goal was never to be a symbol of healing, just a human being who made it through and chose to reach back when I could.

Now, when I share, it's from overflow, not obligation. From wholeness, not pressure. From choice, not guilt.

And that's when it started healing me again, too.

There were times advocacy felt heavier than healing. I thought speaking out, sharing my story, and helping others would lift me. I thought telling my truth, being visible and being a voice for those suffering in silence would make me lighter. But some days, it didn't. Some days, it felt like carrying everyone else's pain on top of my own.

I remember sitting in my room after a speaking event or a mental health symposium, the applause still ringing in my ears, people telling me I inspired them. And I felt…empty. Exhausted. Hollow. Because while I was pouring into everybody else, I hadn't poured into myself yet. I was still carrying grief, still wrestling with anger, still haunted by nights I thought I wouldn't wake up. And in those moments, advocacy didn't heal me; it reminded me of all the work I hadn't done inside.

I started noticing a pattern. I was giving so much, sacrificing my rest, my time, my peace to show up for other people. I wanted to be a lifeline, a safe space, a voice for the voiceless, but in doing that, I was running on empty. I was speaking hope I wasn't fully feeling yet. I was offering light while parts of me still felt dark.

It was heavy because it wasn't just about showing up; it was emotional, spiritual, mental labor I hadn't trained for. People expected me to be strong. To have answers. To motivate. To guide. And I wanted to. I really did. But I didn't always feel strong. I didn't always have the answers. Sometimes I didn't even want to talk. But I kept going, thinking that somehow, helping others would fix me.

Eventually, I realized that advocacy doesn't replace healing. Advocacy is powerful, but it's not a substitute for therapy, for rest, for prayer, for processing grief. I had to learn to advocate from a healed place, or at least a healing place. I had to learn boundaries. To speak only when I could give fully without draining myself. To pour into others without forgetting my own cup needed refilling.

The turning point was small but profound. I started asking myself: Who am I helping if I'm breaking in the process? Who can I really lift if I'm barely standing? That's when I gave myself permission to pause. To be silent. To step back. To rebuild myself while still caring for the mission I loved.

Now advocacy feels different. It doesn't feel like a burden. It doesn't feel like a weight on my chest. I still show up, I still speak, I still share my story, but I do it from fullness. From a place where God, therapy, reflection, prayer, and self-care fill me first. And when I show up now, I can finally give without losing pieces of myself in the process.

Advocacy taught me that being a voice for others is sacred, but so is being a voice for yourself. You can't pour from an empty cup. You can't heal others if you're ignoring your own healing. And that was a lesson I had to learn the hard way.

CHAPTER SEVENTEEN

What Grief Taught Me About God

The understanding that grief gave me about God.

CHAPTER SEVENTEEN: What Grief Taught Me About God

The understanding that grief gave me about God.

Grief changed my understanding of God more than any sermon ever did.

Before loss, my faith was mostly answers. Say the right prayers. Believe the right things. Trust that everything happens for a reason I'd one day understand.

God, to me, was certainty.

A plan. A protector. A fixer of things that hurt too much.

Then grief came, and none of those versions of God showed up the way I expected.

The prayers didn't stop the loss.

The faith didn't soften the blow.

The "everything happens for a reason" landed like salt in an open wound.

And for the first time, I didn't want explanations.

I wanted presence.

Grief stripped my faith down to its bones.

I stopped asking, "Why did this happen?"

and started asking, *"Where are You in this?"*

Not in the silver linings.

Not in the lessons.

Not in the forced gratitude.

But in the hospital rooms.

In the empty chairs.

In the quiet after everyone else went home.

Grief taught me that if God is real to me, God has to be able to sit in the dark without rushing me toward the light.

I no longer see God as the one who orchestrates pain to teach me something. I see God as the one who stays when pain makes everything else leave.

In the friend who didn't try to fix it.

In the stranger who held the door when my hands were full of flowers I never wanted to buy.

In the moments I felt completely shattered, but somehow still held.

Grief made my faith less polished and more honest.

Grief taught me a lot about God. Some of it I didn't want to learn at the time, some of it I had to wrestle through kicking and screaming, and some of it surprised me with its quiet truth.

First, grief taught me that God is bigger than my understanding. I spent days, weeks, months asking "Why?", why my grandma, why my friends, why my family, why me? I wanted answers I couldn't get, and for a long time, I thought silence meant He didn't care. But grief forced me to see that maybe His silence wasn't absence, it was presence in a way I couldn't see. God doesn't always explain in the moment, but He's always there, holding, guiding, and waiting for us to trust Him even when we don't understand.

Grief also taught me that God can carry me through more than I thought possible. I didn't know I had that much pain in me. I didn't know I could feel so empty, so hopeless, and still keep breathing. But He kept me alive. He kept me showing up for myself even when I wanted to shut the world out. Every tear, every sleepless night, every angry thought, I made it through because He was there carrying the weight I couldn't carry alone.

Grief taught me about His timing, and more importantly, about patience, both His and mine. I wanted healing on my schedule. I wanted closure immediately. I wanted my life to feel "normal" again in a week, a month, maybe a year. Grief taught me that healing doesn't have a timer. God doesn't rush, and neither should I. Each step, no matter how small, mattered. And even when it felt like nothing was happening, He was working in ways I couldn't see.

Grief taught me that God is tender. He's not just powerful, He's gentle. He meets you where you are, not where He wants you to be. He didn't lecture me about faith or shame me for being angry. He didn't take the pain away instantly. He just sat with me in it, quietly, patiently, without forcing me to "get over it." And I learned that sometimes, His tenderness is the loudest thing in the world.

Grief taught me that God doesn't leave us in the dark forever. He uses pain to draw us closer, to reveal His faithfulness, to show us the beauty of resilience. I saw Him in people who came through when I needed them, in moments of clarity when I felt lost, in the small joys that reminded me life could still be beautiful. Even in the darkest nights, He was there. Even when I didn't feel Him, He was working behind the scenes.

Grief taught me that God is trustworthy. I didn't feel like trusting Him at first. I was mad. I was hurt. I doubted. I questioned everything I had been taught about Him. But through it all, He proved that He is faithful even when I am not. Even when I couldn't see it, even when I didn't believe it, even when I wanted to give up on life and faith alike, He never left me.

And finally, grief taught me that God can turn pain into purpose. I've taken every tear, every sleepless night, every "why me" moment, and turned it into something that can help others. I speak. I advocate. I encourage. I write. I share. My grief didn't just break me, it built me. And God's hand was all over that rebuilding. He took my brokenness and showed me how it could be used to help, to inspire, to save, even just one person feeling alone in the world.

Grief didn't make me question God forever. It made me question what I thought I knew about Him. And through that questioning, I learned more about Him than I ever could have without pain. Grief taught me that God is real, God is present, God is tender, God is patient, and most of all, God is love that never leaves, even when everything else does.

A God I meet in tears, in memory, in love that doesn't end just because a life did. A God who feels closer in my breaking than in my certainty.

Grief didn't take all of my faith away.

It changed it.

Deepened it.

Made it wide enough to hold both sorrow and hope in the same trembling hands.

CHAPTER EIGHTEEN

Waking Up Means I'm Not Done

Rebuilding. Rediscovering purpose. Seeing each morning as a reminder that I'm chosen.

CHAPTER EIGHTEEN: Waking Up Means I'm Not Done

Rebuilding. Rediscovering purpose. Seeing each morning as a reminder that I'm chosen.

A Quiet Miracle Every Morning

Every morning is a quiet miracle. The alarm rings. The sun rises. And here I am, still breathing, still alive, still got another chance. Some days it feels ordinary, almost invisible. But I've learned that waking up is a declaration: I'm not done. Not yet. Not ever. God has chosen me to tell His story, how He brought me out of darkness and how He got the glory out of my situation. There were seasons when morning felt like a punishment, a reminder of what I had lost and how broken I felt inside. I would stare at the ceiling, wishing I could hit pause on life itself. But slowly, through prayer, reflection, and small acts of courage, I began to see mornings differently. Each sunrise became a reminder that I was chosen, that my life still had meaning, and that rebuilding was possible.

A Fresh Chance to Try Again, Purpose Isn't Perfection

Waking up doesn't erase the pain. It doesn't suddenly fill the void or make yesterday's struggles disappear. But it's a chance, a fresh canvas, to reclaim your purpose, to take one small step toward the life you're meant to live. Each day is a permission slip to try again, to love again, to speak again, and to trust again. Rediscovering purpose isn't about perfection. It's about noticing the little ways life asks you to show up, to your faith, to your passions, to yourself. Waking up means you still have a story to write, still have lessons to learn, and still have someone to inspire, even if that someone is just you.

Seeing Purpose in the Spotlight

There was the thrill of walking the red carpet at movie premieres and the BET Awards. At first, it felt surreal, like a dream I wasn't sure I deserved. But amidst the flashing cameras and excitement, I realized something deeper. These weren't just celebrations of my career; they were proof that showing up, even when life felt impossible, leads to opportunities to inspire. Each step, each handshake, each smile meant that my story mattered, and that gave me purpose.

When Purpose Became Service

But the moments that truly touched my heart deeply were when Teh'ja, who is now my good sister who I love deeply, and I will forever be thankful for the opportunity. She invited me to have a mental health week to speak to her students in Chicago at Gary Comer Middle School. I walked into rooms full of kids, unsure of what I could teach them. Then I saw their eyes, wide and searching, mirroring pieces of my own journey. As I shared my story, my struggles, and my hope, something shifted. Students and teachers began to open up, and some even broke down in tears, finally feeling seen and understood. Some shared that they can't even talk to their parents about their mental health issues. That day, I realized my pain wasn't wasted. My journey wasn't just survival; it was service. By showing up authentically, I could help others find their voice, their courage, their hope, and find God and give Him a try. And JazLynn Smith. My friend, my sister, since the 6th grade. Whenever her students are going through things mentally, and she wants them to be reminded that there's hope in the midst of their challenges, she calls me every time. She'll say, "Bro, I need you. My girls are going through it. Do you think you can come up here?" And I showed up every time for her, and I will always be a call away. It just reassures me that my story is and will help so many people overcome, and that's all I really want.

Seeing Myself In Tyler Perry

I remember this night like it was yesterday. It was one of those seasons in my life when I felt completely lost. I was questioning everything about my career and the path I was on. Did I still want to act? Was I really doing what God called me to do? Would I ever live the dreams that God placed inside of me? My mind was full of questions, and honestly, I felt hopeless. Then one day, I watched *Maxine's Baby: The Tyler Perry Story*. And when I tell you that documentary did something to me, it really did. Watching the journey of Tyler Perry, seeing everything he went through growing up and the man he became, gave me a level of hope I didn't even realize I needed. It motivated me and reminded me that what God promises, He always has a way of bringing it to pass. I remember sitting there crying after it ended because I saw so much of myself in his story. I saw the pain, the struggle, the doubt, but I also saw the purpose. And in that moment, I was reminded of something powerful: my pain doesn't define me. What I choose to do with it does. I've been a fan of Tyler Perry since I was a jit, probably around five years old, watching his plays. But this time it felt different. This time, his story didn't just entertain me; it woke something up inside of me. It reminded me that my story matters too… and maybe everything I've been through is just the beginning of what God is about to do in my life.

Still Chosen, Still Not Done

So waking up each morning became, and still is, a reminder of this truth: I'm not done. My life is a message, and every sunrise is an invitation to continue writing it. Every challenge, every heartbreak, every tear I've shed has been part of the path that leads me to purpose and to the people I'm meant to touch.

CHAPTER NINETEEN

Chosen by Pain, Controlled by Expectations

The pressure of living up to family, society, and the world's expectations while silently battling pain and trying not to lose myself.

CHAPTER NINETEEN: Chosen by Pain, Controlled by Expectations

The pressure of living up to family, society, and the world's expectations while silently battling pain and trying not to lose myself.

Growing up, nobody really teaches you how heavy expectations can become.

Sometimes they don't even look like pressure at first. Sometimes it sounds like love. *"You gotta be successful." "Make us proud." "Be strong." "Don't mess up."* And before you know it, you start building your life around what everybody else expects from you instead of what you actually need for yourself.

I spent a lot of time trying to live up to expectations, family expectations, society's expectations, and even expectations from people who didn't understand my story. The expectation to always be strong. The expectation to smile through pain. The expectation to have it all together when inside, I was struggling.

The truth is, carrying everybody else's expectations almost made me lose myself.

I wanted to be accepted. I wanted people to be proud of me. I wanted validation so badly that I started sacrificing my peace trying to become the version of myself everybody else wanted. But what happens when the version they want isn't the real you?

That question changed everything for me.

Because while I was busy trying to make everybody else comfortable, I was uncomfortable. While I was trying to make everybody proud, I was silently battling pain, pressure, overthinking, and mental exhaustion. I learned that living for other people's approval can become a prison.

And one of the hardest lessons I had to learn was realizing how often people expect you to show up for them without ever considering what you may be carrying yourself.

People wanted me to be there for them. To encourage them, support them, help them, listen to them, and somehow still remain strong through it all. People wanted access to my energy, my time, and my presence, but very few stopped to ask, *"How are you really doing?"*

Nobody really asked what I was carrying.

Nobody really asked what I was struggling with.

Nobody really asked if I was okay.

And if they did, sometimes it felt like they weren't prepared for the honest answer.

That part hurt more than I can explain.

Because when you're the strong one, people get comfortable with your strength. They expect you to always show up, always have the answers, always pour into them, all while ignoring the fact that you might be empty too. They expect you to carry their problems while silently carrying your own.

The truth is, constantly pouring into others while neglecting yourself will drain you. Especially when you're already trying to survive mentally.

The world has expectations, too.

Social media tells us who we should be. Success has deadlines that people try to place on us. Family can unknowingly pass down pressure from generations before us. Sometimes people project their unfulfilled dreams onto you, and if you're not careful, you'll spend years chasing a life that was never truly yours.

That pressure is real.

And if we're being honest, it's exhausting.

Especially when you're already trying to survive mentally.

There came a point where I had to ask myself: Am I living in purpose, or am I living in pressure?

That question forced me to be honest.

I realized healing meant disappointing some people. Growth meant saying NO. Purpose meant finally listening to myself and to God more than outside opinions. I had to stop chasing approval and start choosing peace. I had to stop overextending myself for people who didn't always check on me the way I checked on them. I had to learn that protecting my peace wasn't selfish; it was necessary.

Because the truth is this:

You can make everybody happy and still be miserable.

You can meet every expectation and still feel empty.

You can constantly show up for people and still feel unseen.

You can become who the world wants and completely lose who you are.

Healing started when I gave myself permission to stop performing. To stop pretending. And to stop carrying what was never mine.

I had to learn that my purpose wasn't to become who everybody expected me to be. My purpose was to become who I was created to be.

And maybe that's where freedom starts.

Not in perfection.

Not in approval.

But in finally choosing yourself.

CHAPTER TWENTY

This Is Heart Work

Closing Reflection, Letters and Prayers

Closing Reflection

I started this book searching for healing, not knowing what I would find. Along the way, I learned that healing isn't a destination. It's a rhythm, a return, a constant coming home to yourself.

There are still hard days. There are still moments when the weight feels heavy. But now I know how to hold it differently, with patience, with softness, with the understanding that broken doesn't mean beyond repair.

I've learned that speaking your truth doesn't make you weak: It makes you free. And every time we choose honesty over silence, we make room for someone else to breathe too.

If you've made it to this page, thank you for walking beside me, for seeing me, and maybe for seeing yourself in these words.

This isn't the end of the story. It's just another beginning. One written in peace, in purpose, and in the quiet strength of survival.

A Letter to My Grandma

Dear Grandma Sharon,

I miss you more than words can explain. Some days it still feels unreal, like if I close my eyes long enough, I'll wake up and you'll be right there. Other days, the reality hits me all over again, and I feel the same ache I felt when you first left. I wish I could tell you how hard it was to learn how to live without you. It's still hard, but I'm still doing the best I can. I made it this far, so I know I'm on the right path.

There were so many moments I needed you and didn't know where to put that need. I needed your voice, your prayers, your presence. I needed the comfort I used to feel just knowing you were here. Losing you changed me in ways I'm still learning to understand.

I want you to know that there were times I didn't think I was going to make it. Times when the grief was so heavy it felt like it was crushing me. I was angry. I was lost. I questioned everything. But even in those moments, something in me kept thinking about you. About your strength. About your faith. About your love. About how you never gave up.

I carry you with me in ways people can't see. In the way I love. In the way I pray. I keep going even when it's hard. I hope I'm making you proud. I hope you see me pushing through, trying to turn my pain into purpose.

I love you forever. And no matter how much time passes, you will FOREVER be a part of me.

I Love always and FOREVER,
Your Grandson JuneJune

A Letter to God (During the Darkest Night)

God,

This is the night I didn't know if I trusted You anymore. I was tired of being strong. Tired of praying and still hurting. Tired of feeling like I was talking to the ceiling. I didn't have fancy words or faith-filled sentences, just frustration, confusion, and pain.

I asked You why. Why me? Why this much loss? Why this kind of silence? I didn't understand how You could see me hurting and not stop it. I felt abandoned, even though I knew You were supposed to be near.

That night, I wasn't praising You. I was questioning You. I wasn't confident; I was broken. I didn't feel hopeful. I felt empty. But somehow, even in my anger, I still talked to You. And maybe that was faith, even when it didn't feel like it.

You didn't fix everything that night. You didn't explain anything. But You didn't let me go either. You sat with me in the dark. You kept me alive when I didn't care if I was here anymore.

Looking back, I see it now. You were holding me together when I was falling apart. Even when I didn't feel You, You were there. And for that, I'm thankful. I'm still here because You didn't give up on me when I was ready to give up on everything.

A Letter to the Version of Me That Almost Gave Up

To the me who almost quit,

I know how tired you were. I know how heavy everything felt. I know how close you came to walking away from it all. You didn't want to die; you just wanted the pain to stop.

You felt alone even in rooms full of people. You felt misunderstood, unseen, unheard. You carried more than anyone knew, and you did it quietly. I need you to know something: you weren't weak. You were overwhelmed.

I'm proud of you for holding on, even when you didn't know why you should. I'm proud of you for surviving days you never thought you'd get through. You kept breathing when everything inside you wanted to quit.

If you could see me now, you'd see that staying was worth it. Life didn't magically get easy, but it got real. It was meaningful. You found purpose in the pain. You found your voice. You found God in a deeper way.

Thank you for not giving up. Thank you for staying. We made it further than you ever thought we would.

A Letter To My Current Self

You've come a long way, further than you ever thought you could. There were nights you didn't think you'd make it, days when getting out of bed felt impossible. But you did it anyway. You kept going, even when the light felt out of reach. Even when everyone left you in the midst of it all, you kept fighting and found your way through the dark.

You carried pain that no one else could see, and yet you never stopped searching for meaning in it. You kept showing up for yourself, for your healing, for the life you deserve.

I know you still have days where the weight feels heavy. That's okay. Healing was never supposed to mean you'd stop feeling; it just means you've learned how to hold those feelings with care. You've learned how to give yourself grace.

I'm proud of you! Not because you've figured everything out, but because you've learned to be honest with yourself. You've learned to rest without guilt, to cry without shame, and to love yourself through the process.

In the midst of your pain, grief and hurt, you still went after your dreams and all the things you said you were gonna get. You haven't been everywhere around the globe yet, but you've been everywhere that you said you wanted to go. You were in pain during some of those trips, but you showed up. That's why I'm proud of you.

You don't owe the world perfection. You only owe yourself peace.

Keep choosing you, even when it's hard. Keep believing that your story matters, because it does. You do.

With Love,

Me

A Letter to Someone Reading This Who Is Suicidal or Grieving

To you,

If you're reading this and hurting, I want you to know you're not alone. I know what it feels like to wake up tired of waking up. I know what it feels like to miss someone so much it physically hurts. I know what it's like to smile for people while breaking inside.

You might feel like nobody really understands what you're going through. You might feel like the pain will never end. You might feel like giving up is the only way to find peace. But please hear me when I say this: you matter. Your life matters.

The pain you're feeling right now is real, but it is not the end of your story. This chapter is heavy, but it's not the whole book. Even when you can't see a way forward, there is still hope. I promise you, there is more life waiting for you than you can imagine.

Please stay. Talk to someone. Cry if you need to. Ask for help. Lean on God, even if all you can say is "I'm tired." You don't have to be strong right now; you just have to keep going.

The world is better with you in it. And one day, you'll look back and realize that surviving this moment was one of the bravest things you ever did.

You are loved. You are seen. And you are not alone.

A Letter To The Reader

Dear reader,

If you're reading this, you made it to this moment, and that means something. Maybe more than you know.

This book isn't polished pain. It's not tied up with a pretty bow or filtered to make it easier to digest. It's real. It's raw. It's everything I've held in, cried through, prayed over, and survived. It's my truth, unapologetic and unedited.

This book isn't just my story. It's a reminder that survival is strength, vulnerability is courage, and healing is not a destination. It's a daily act of self-love. You have every right to take up space, to speak your truth, and to rebuild your life on your own terms.

This book is my way of saying: You're not crazy. You're not weak. And you're definitely not alone.

There will be days when doubt tries to silence your voice, when old wounds whisper that you haven't changed. But remember this: you already have. Every step you've taken toward yourself is proof of your resilience.

Keep choosing you. Keep rising. Keep believing that your story matters, because it does. And the world needs the light only you can give.

I hope you saw your own pain in these pages. But I also hope you see your power. I hope this book reminds you that healing is messy, that progress doesn't always look like peace, and that surviving is something to be proud of.

Read it when you need a reminder that surviving is a win. Healing isn't always pretty, and it sure as hell isn't linear. But you don't have to do it perfectly, you just have to keep going.

Wherever you are in your journey, please remember that you matter. Your story matters. Your existence is not an accident; it's a masterpiece still in progress.

You're not broken. You're becoming.

With all my heart,

Marlon Qualls Jr.

Special Acknowledgment & Dedication to Dr. Sarita

Dr. Sarita, I don't know if words can ever truly capture the depth of my gratitude, but I want to try. You met me in my darkest moments, when grief felt like it would swallow me whole, and you walked with me patiently, gently, and without judgment. You helped me name my pain, face my fears, and find pieces of myself I thought were lost forever.

You didn't just counsel me, you saw me. You held space for my tears, my doubts, and my raw, messy humanity, and in doing so, you reminded me that healing is possible. You showed me how to grieve without shame, to hope without apology, and to trust even when it felt impossible.

Because of you, I've learned that it's okay to be vulnerable, that my story matters, and that God's love can meet me even in the deepest valleys. Your guidance, your wisdom, and your heart have changed my life in ways I will carry forever. Thank you for listening without judgment, for walking beside me through the darkness, and for gently reminding me of hope when I couldn't see it myself. Your impact on my journey is immeasurable, and I am forever grateful.

I am endlessly grateful for you, Dr. Sarita, and for the gift of your presence in my journey. I wouldn't be here if it wasn't for you. I know I would have given up. You helped and encouraged me to get closer and build a stronger relationship with God. You will always have a special place in my heart. I love you and thank God for you!

Closing Prayer

God,

Thank You for carrying me through every chapter of my life, especially the ones I didn't think I would survive. Thank You for staying close when I was angry, confused, and hurting. Thank You for hearing my prayers even when all I could offer You was silence, tears, or frustration.

Thank You for keeping me alive on the nights I wanted the pain to end. Thank You for protecting me when I didn't know how to protect myself. Thank You for loving me when I didn't love myself and for never walking away, even when I felt like walking away from everything.

I thank You for the healing that has already happened and for the healing that's still in progress. Thank You for reminding me that healing isn't a destination, it's a journey, and that You walk with me every step of the way. Thank You for turning my pain into purpose and my story into something that can help others feel less alone.

God, I pray for everyone who reads these words. For the ones who are grieving, hurting, or barely holding on. Cover them. Comfort them. Remind them that they are seen, loved, and not forgotten. Give them strength for today and hope for tomorrow, even if it comes one breath at a time.

Help us to trust You when we don't understand. Help us to choose faith over fear, obedience over opinion, and love over bitterness. Keep our hearts soft in a hard world and our spirits grounded in Your truth.

I place everything in Your hands, my past, my present, and my future. Thank You for not being finished with me yet.

In Jesus' name,

Amen.

You Are Not Alone

If you're reading this and life feels heavy right now, If your thoughts won't slow down or If you feel like giving up...

Please hear this clearly: You are not alone. There are real people ready to listen, support you, and help you through this moment.

🚨 NEED HELP RIGHT NOW?

Call or Text: 988 (Suicide & Crisis Lifeline) – 24/7, Free, Confidential

💬 TALK TO SOMEONE

Text HOME to 741741 (Crisis Text Line)

□ VETERANS

Call or text 988, then press 1

🏠 ABUSE / DOMESTIC VIOLENCE

1-800-799-7233

⚠ SEXUAL ASSAULT

1-800-656-4673

🌈 LGBTQ+ SUPPORT

1-866-488-7386

🏃‍♂️RUN AWAY YOUTH / TEENS

1-800-786-2929

🍽 EATING DISORDERS

Call or Text: (866) 662-1235

🍺 SUBSTANCE USE / ADDICTION

1-800-662-4357

Reaching out is not weakness. It's strength. Even if you don't know what to say. Just start. *If you are in immediate danger, call 911.*

www.ingramcontent.com/pod-product-compliance
Ingram Content Group UK Ltd.
Pitfield, Milton Keynes, MK11 3LW, UK
UKHW022025041026
15591UKWH00012B/489

9 798996 424047